Excerpts from two of the stories:

From "Yecenia"

"I read the book *Frankenstein* and felt sorry for the monster. I thought of how it was like the Latino community," Yecenia says. "The media really presents us unfairly—whenever you see a Latino person on the news or TV, it's always something negative, something bad. We're often pre-judged. Like when people find out I'm from South Central L.A., they automatically stereotype me and put me down. But they know nothing about me."

From "Diego"

"I just knew. I knew I didn't want to mess up my life. So I stopped hanging out with that group of kids."

Eighteen-year-old Diego is thinking back to a time that, in years, was not that long ago. But in experience, it seems like a lifetime ago. As a ten-year-old in West New York, New Jersey, just across the Hudson River from Manhattan, Diego remembers a lot of what he calls "little street gangs." These were groups of young boys, not much older than 10 or 12, who were just beginning to test their ability to get into trouble. Diego began roaming around with some of these boys when he was 10.

La Vida Real

*True Stories
of Latino
Students Today*

•••

TANYA SAVORY

 THE TOWNSEND LIBRARY

LA VIDA REAL

TP THE TOWNSEND LIBRARY

For more titles in the Townsend Library,
visit our website: www.townsendpress.com

Townsend Press, Inc.
439 Kelley Drive
West Berlin, NJ 08091
cs@townsendpress.com

ISBN-13: 978-1-59194-179-8
ISBN-10: 1-59194-179-2

Library of Congress Control Number:
2008937881

CONTENTS

Introduction

It's true that human emotions and feelings are the same regardless of what one's race might be. Why, then, a book specifically about Latino young people and students? While feelings such as fear, joy, anger, and love may be no different just because a person is Latino, experiences and stories often are unique and different.

Today, Latinos make up the largest minority group in the United States. It is not always easy being a member of a minority, particularly if one is just learning the culture and customs of a new country. Sometimes it can make a person feel as though he or she doesn't fit in or that what he or she has to offer isn't important. However, the true stories presented in this book prove otherwise. From the teen mother who battles and eventually overcomes the deadly lure of drugs and gang membership, to the high school senior who discovers the touching truth about his immigrant grandfather—each personal story is very important. And so is each person who tells his or her story.

While all of the stories you are about to read are true, some of the names and locations of those telling the stories have been changed or omitted. This is particularly true when the individual telling his or her story presents details that are deeply personal or painful. Other times, the person telling the story may refer to relatives that are not legal residents of the United States. In any event, the privacy of those who have been generous enough to provide their stories but do not wish to reveal their identities has been respected. Yecenia and Diego, who agreed to share their photos as well as their stories are pictured on the front cover of the book.

These are, of course, only a handful of countless other stories of Latino lives throughout the United States—real human stories still waiting to be told.

Alvara

"It was so dark in the desert. There was no moon at all that night. One really clear memory I have is of my mother telling me not to sit down on the big flat rocks. The rocks were still warm from the day, so that's where the rattlesnakes slept." Alvara doesn't make eye contact when she talks about the night she and her mother joined twenty-four others in the small border town of Naco in Sonora, Mexico, for what she simply refers to as "the crossing."

3

"There's a Naco on both sides of the border—one in Arizona and one in Mexico," Alvara explains. "That's how it got its name: *na* from the end of 'Arizona' and *co* from the end of 'Mexico.'"

And on that night in 1996 when Alvara was ten years old, she held her mother's hand tightly as the quiet group huddled together outside of an old hotel. The rundown and mostly boarded-up hotel was a common meeting spot for those who were planning to cross the Mexican/United States border illegally.

"We had to wait for a coyote to lead us to a safe place to cross," Alvara continues. "There are a few miles of a tall wall that separates the two Nacos. And there are lots of border patrols right in that area. But a little further out . . ."

Here, Alvara's voice trails off as she thinks back to that night. A "coyote" is a paid guide who knows the paths and trails that are safest to follow. He knows where the wall turns into a simple barbed-wire fence. And he knows where the holes in the fences are. Coyotes are paid a lot of money for their services—sometimes more than $1,000 per person. Most of those being guided by the coyote are quite poor and must borrow from, or be given the money by, a friend or relative already in the U.S.

"My father had already been in the United States for almost two years, working very hard to save money so that we could all be together.

He worked two and sometimes three different jobs. During the day he did landscaping, and then he was on the line at a meat-packing factory at night." Alvara pauses, a flash of anger darkening her face.

"You know, I often hear people say that what my father did, and then what my mother and I did . . . that we were wrong. We are criminals, some people say. But anyone who says that just doesn't know." Alvara takes a deep breath, trying to calm her emotions. "We didn't have a choice. That's just a fact. It was either stay and starve or take our chances coming north. You can see—we didn't have a choice."

Alvara was born in a rural village in the state of Oaxaca in southern coastal Mexico. Home was a roughly constructed adobe building with a thin roof that leaked when it rained. The floors were dirt, and there was no electricity and no plumbing. The "kitchen" for many people in the community was a stone oven and fire in the middle of the village. Every day, women of the village would meet to put together enough food for everyone to have at least one meal a day. That meal usually consisted of tortillas and a bowl of beans. Alvara's family was fortunate enough to have their own stone oven and fireplace in their home.

Alvara was also luckier than many of the children in the village. Most of the children began working before they were even ten years old. But

Alvara's parents made sure that their daughter attended school.

"No education means you stay poor. That's what my parents always said. Neither of my parents even finished third grade, so they knew what they were talking about," Alvara says. "They could read and write, but just barely."

The school Alvara attended was constructed of four poles holding up a palm-leaf roof. Students of all ages sat together in a circle, stumps and rocks serving as chairs. But as rough as the surroundings were, Alvara was glad to be there. Her teacher was patient and generous, often spending his own money to supply students with the very few books, sheets of paper, and pencils they had. Alvara learned to read and write, and she even learned some basic English. Little did she know at the time how valuable this skill would become one day.

Alvara's father owned a fairly large bean field, but the soil was generally too rocky to get very good crops. Even though he worked from sunrise until dark, he rarely earned more than three dollars a day. This was barely enough to feed and take care of the family, but somehow Alvara and her parents managed to scrape by. However, one warm October night, something happened that destroyed even the small bit of security the family had.

"Since we were near the coast, we had lived through hurricanes before," Alvara remembers.

"But this one was like nothing we had ever seen. It just flattened everything."

In 1997, Hurricane Pauline hit Oaxaca with its full force. Winds of more than 100 miles an hour tore through the small villages and towns. More than sixteen inches of rain in some areas caused severe flooding. More destructive than the winds and rain were the horrible mudslides. Hundreds of people were killed when entire hillsides collapsed, slid, and buried entire communities. But Alvara's parents were wise. Unlike a number of their neighbors, they heeded the warnings about how dangerous this hurricane would be and took shelter inside a safe building in a nearby town. Huddled with dozens of other families inside the unlit brick building, Alvara remembers hearing the wind outside.

"It was shrieking and really spooky. Every now and then we would hear something hit the outside of the building with a big thump. Everyone just sat together holding hands and praying. It seemed like it went on forever, but I guess it was only a few hours."

The next morning, Alvara walked with her parents up the hill and toward their village. It was a difficult walk through debris, fallen trees, and deep water in many spots. When they reached the village, what they saw shocked them. Hardly anything was left standing. But the most bizarre sight was the heavy mud that had entirely covered the western side of the village, where the wind and rain had been strongest.

"It looked like a bomb had gone off or something. You could see a few trees sticking out of the mud, but that was about all . . . except . . ." Alvara remembers with a shake of her head. "My mother tried to keep me from seeing it, but twice I saw arms reaching out from the mud—arms of dead people. You could tell they had been trying to crawl out. It was like a nightmare."

And the bean field, Alvara's family's only source of income, had been completely destroyed. Mud and water had washed away all the plants, and now the field was nothing more than a rocky pit.

"I was pretty young, so I didn't understand exactly how bad it all was. But I remember looking at my father, and he had never looked so scared. I think he knew right away that we would have to do something drastic."

One year later, Alvara's father, Hernan, was living with several other men in a small apartment outside of Louisville, Kentucky. Hernan had had a close friend from childhood who had crossed the border into Arizona several years earlier. He had found seasonal work on farms throughout the Southwest, and eventually he heard about higher-paying construction jobs in Kentucky. This is where he had lived now for three years.

Hernan had always kept in touch with his

friend. In letters, his friend let him know that there was plenty of work, and that Hernan could stay with him if he ever decided to make the crossing. And most importantly, his friend told him he would lend him the money to pay the coyote at the border. *You will either get caught, or you will die in the desert if you don't have a coyote to show you the way*, Hernan's friend had once written. *Don't try to do this alone!*

And so, a few weeks after the hurricane, Hernan had written to his friend. For a while, Alvara and her parents had been living in a shelter provided by the Mexican Red Cross, but those days would be coming to an end. Nearly penniless, his home and land destroyed, and with no opportunities for work in his homeland, Hernan was desperate. He didn't like the idea of entering the United States illegally, but he could not just stand by and watch his daughter and wife go hungry. As any parent would, Hernan wanted a better life for his daughter.

"My father still believes that we would have been forced to beg in the streets if we had stayed," Alvara says quietly. "And the education that he and my mother demanded I receive was no longer available after the storm. If anything, my life would have been worse than my parents' lives if we had stayed. My father, particularly, would not stand for that."

Hernan borrowed money from his friend to cross the border, and then he hitchhiked to

Kentucky, mostly getting rides from truckers. Alvara recalls that her father knew next to no English, but, thankfully, he had learned "Louisville" and "Kentucky" so that the rides would take him in the right direction. When he arrived in Louisville, his friend had already lined up some work. But Hernan would need to work two and sometimes three jobs to repay his friend, send money to his wife and daughter, pay his own bills, *and* save enough money to pay another coyote to lead Alvara and her mother across the border.

"My mother would read me the letters my father sent, and he often wrote that he didn't sleep more than a few hours a night. But then he'd always say that all the work would be worth it in the end. It would just take time."

And finally the time came. Alvara's mother received the one thousand dollars it would cost to pay the coyote. There was also money for the bus rides from Oaxaca to the Mexican/United States border and then from Arizona to Kentucky. It would be a very long journey for a ten-year-old girl—particularly a ten-year-old girl who had never been more than twenty miles from her home.

"It was more than 1,500 miles just to get to the border. We just slept and lived on the bus for three days. We'd stop in little towns along the way for food or to pick up and drop off other travelers. Twice, we had to switch buses. Mostly I remember it being hot, but not boring. Since I'd never traveled anywhere, everything was new and interesting to me," Alvara recalls. "But even so, I guess I was ready to get off that bus after three days!"

The bus arrived at Naco, Sonora, Mexico in the middle of the afternoon. A dozen or more people were already sitting in the shade of the old hotel. Many of them held sacks of food and belongings, and everyone had one or two gallons of water in plastic jugs at their sides. Most were men, but there were also other women and children. Standing on the corners near the hotel, young men in dark sunglasses stood smoking and watching the group carefully. Every now and then, those who were waiting would wander over to one of the young men and talk quietly.

"These were the coyotes," Alvara explains. "People would talk to them, agree on a price, and find out when we'd be leaving. It was all done in a real quiet way, but not really hidden since, you know, there's no law against talking to a stranger. My mother talked to one, and then she and I walked over to the small store down the street to buy supplies. I kept asking why. Why did we need supplies? For what? My mother wouldn't really explain what we were going to have to do—probably because she thought it would scare me. And looking back, she was right."

The Sonoran Desert stretches up from Sonora, Mexico into Arizona. It is such a desolate, hot, and often deadly area of land that Spanish explorers in the 1500s named it *El Camino del Diablo*—The Devil's Highway. For as far as anyone can see, there is nothing but rock bluffs, lava stone, prickly cactus, dust, and sand. In the summer, temperatures can soar as high as 130 degrees, and since there are no trees, there is no place to escape the scorching sun and heat.

It would be into this desert that Alvara and her mother would walk with the rest of their group for many miles. Once across the border, the closest highway was nearly twenty-five miles away. The coyote had arranged for vans to pick up the travelers at a designated point along the rarely-traveled highway. But they would have to get there on foot.

"People used to cross the border closer to cities, like from Tijuana to San Diego or from Juarez to El Paso. Once they were across, it was easy to find work nearby or transportation to somewhere else. But now, those areas are so closely patrolled that it's hard to cross without getting caught. Out in a big empty area like the desert, people don't get caught as often—but, then, there are other dangers."

Just after dark, the coyote that Alvara's mother had spoken to gathered his group together. He spoke quickly and quietly about where they were headed, what to expect, and how extremely important it was for everyone to stick together. Then he led everyone down a dark dirt road, then onto a faint path, and then into the desert. The group walked silently for two miles until the few lights of Naco, Mexico disappeared completely. The only sounds were a high, whistling wind far out in the desert and the faint howling of coyotes (*real* coyotes) in the distance. Suddenly, the group made a sharp turn as they headed toward the border.

After a few more miles, the coyote stopped at an old wire fence. It was nearly six feet high, but part of it had been cut so that it could be pulled aside to create an opening just big enough for a person to squeeze through. As the coyote held the fencing aside, everyone slipped through one by one.

"I remember thinking, 'That was easy.' But I guess I still hadn't understood that we were going to have to walk half the night and part of the next day," Alvara says with a smile. "I thought that as soon as we crossed the border, everything would suddenly change."

Alvara held on to her mother's hand that entire night as the group made its way across the eerie desert. The coyote followed a very old path—one that may have been used even hundreds of years ago by natives, back before there were borders or separate countries. It was hard to see the path in the darkness, but every now and then Alvara would see discarded water bottles, wrappers, or even clothing. It was clear that many people from Mexico had traveled this very same route.

Late into the night, the group stopped to rest for a few hours, huddling together in the chilly air of a desert night. But before the sun rose, they were back on the old path.

"We were pretty fortunate," Alvara remembers. "It was still only May, so the desert was not terribly hot yet. When the sun finally did come up, it only got into the upper 80s. Since I've gotten older, I've heard some horrible stories. Hundreds and hundreds of people have died trying to cross that desert during the summer months. They run out of water, and then the desert just fries them. They roll around in the sand, trying to escape the sun. It's a very painful way to die."

Before noon, Alvara and her mother hid with the rest of the group behind large boulders near an empty two-lane gravel road. Within thirty minutes, two vans that would carry everyone to Tucson pulled up in a cloud of dust. A two-hour drive to Tucson, a long wait in a filthy bus station, and then a three-day bus ride from Tucson to Kentucky seemed like forever to a ten-year-old girl.

"I remember looking out the window of the bus at all these new things I had never seen before. It was amazing to me. I knew then that

I wasn't just headed to meet my father. I was heading into a new life."

When Alvara and her mother finally reached the Louisville bus station, they were dusty, exhausted, and wearing the same wrinkled clothes they had worn for many days. As they pulled into the station, Hernan came running out and jogged alongside the bus, waving and grinning until it came to a stop.

"I hadn't seen my dad in over two years, but the second I saw him running alongside the bus, it was like we'd never been apart," Alvara recalls with a shy smile. "My mother had been worried about looking so bad, but when Dad saw us, it was like we were the two most beautiful women in the world. He grabbed us when we got off the bus, and he started crying. I'd never seen my father cry before that, and I've never seen him cry since. He was just so happy to see us again."

Twelve years later, Alvara is a thoughtful, well-spoken, and determined young woman. Her memories of the crossing bring up mixed feelings. She is proud of what her parents went through to create a better life, but she is troubled by the fact that her parents are still illegal immigrants. Although Alvara was also an illegal immigrant when she first came to the United States, she recently gained legal status when she married a citizen of the United States.

"My mother and father live in constant fear of being sent back to Mexico," she explains. "They are proud and happy to be here, but they often feel as though they have to hide. They want to learn English, but they think that if they go to a class, they will get arrested."

But in spite of their fear, Alvara's parents feel that every sacrifice they've made and continue to make is worth the one dream they had for their daughter—an education. Although her first few years in school here were difficult, Alvara worked hard and eventually graduated from high school near the top of her class.

"I know a lot of people think it's unfair for children of illegal immigrants to be allowed to receive an education. But I've never understood how it would make things *more* fair to deny learning to anyone. That just doesn't make sense."

Today, Alvara is taking classes at a local community college and hoping to transfer to a four-year school before long. Some day, she would like to receive a degree in immigration law.

"There are so many questions, so many problems when it comes to immigration. There are a lot of changes to be made, and a lot of people to help." Alvara pauses, possibly thinking back to that strange night so many years ago. Then she smiles and simply says, "I want to do what I can to help."

Tyler

My last name is De Alvilla, and all my relatives for many, many generations came from areas around Mexico City until my grandfather moved to the United States about fifty years ago. But we never spoke Spanish in my family when I was growing up, and my parents named me Tyler so that I'd "fit in" better with everyone else. What they really meant, I think, is that maybe people wouldn't think right away I was Mexican. I know that sounds funny to say, but that's how my parents are. I guess you could say that they're ashamed of their roots. I never thought too much about that until the past year or so. And now it makes me sad for my parents.

I grew up in a mostly white neighborhood in a pretty nice house. My dad wore a suit and tie to work just like everyone else around here, and my mom was always busy with our church and with raising me and my two younger sisters. Mom always dyed her hair blonde, so I can't even imagine what she'd look like with the same dark brown hair my sisters have. There's really nothing about our family, our home, or the way we look that would ever let anyone know for sure that we're Mexican. To me, *that's* the shameful thing. Still, it didn't cross my mind to think about it in that way for a long time. Then last year, when I was a junior in high school, two things happened that made me see things differently.

"The *Bracero* Program" was the title of the chapter we were talking about in our American history class one fall afternoon. I'll admit it—I wasn't really paying very close attention. We were studying a section on Spanish-American history that whole week, so you'd think I might have been kind of interested. But like I said, I never really thought of myself as Latino too much. But then, as we turned through the pages, something caught my eye. It was a picture of a farming tool known as a "short handle hoe." My grandpa has one just like it sitting on the mantel over his fireplace. He's had it there for as long as I can remember, so it seemed strange to see a picture of the same kind of tool in my history book.

Beneath the hoe was this description: *The*

short hoe was often referred to as an "instrument of horror." The Mexican workers, known as "braceros," were forced to bend over in a painful position in order to use it. Although the farmers could have given the braceros *long hoes, they felt the short hoes did a better job. After ten or twelve hours of this backbreaking work, many* braceros *could not stand up straight. After years of using it, most had permanent spinal damage. This hoe was made illegal in most states by the 1970s, but has remained a symbol of the unjust treatment that many Mexicans endured.*

I remember just sitting there and staring at the picture of that hoe. It's like the rest of the classroom disappeared. I didn't understand. Why did my grandpa have one of these hoes on his mantel? I grew up simply knowing that Grandpa had been a farmer in Texas after he had moved to the United States from Mexico back in the '50s. Now he lived a few blocks away from us in a small apartment. Mostly he just sat on his little front porch watching the neighborhood. Walking around too much was painful—because (and I thought of this with a sudden shock) of his bad back!

That night at dinner, I asked my father, "Was Grandpa a *bracero*?"

My father gave me a funny look and said, "Where did you learn that word?" as though I had just said something bad.

"In school today," I replied. "We were studying about the *Bracero* Program. If that's what Grandpa did, that must have been horrible. It sounds almost like slavery."

My father looked at my mom for a second, and then they both seemed like they were suddenly really interested in dinner. The silence was totally awkward. My two sisters kept looking back and forth from my parents to me. Finally my youngest sister whispered, "Tyler's in trouble!"

"I am *not* in trouble," I said, glaring at my sister. I turned to my mother and then to my father. Neither would look at me. "What? What did I say?"

My father sighed. "Nothing, Tyler. It's just that we prefer to call your grandfather a *farmer*. That's all."

"But he never owned a farm, did he? He was always poor, and he never even—"

"He *worked* on farms. For nearly forty years." My father put his fork down and gave me the look that meant the conversation was over.

It may have been over for him, but it wasn't for me.

My grandpa has lived in his same little cramped apartment ever since Grandma died about eight years ago. They used to own a house way over on the other side of town, but it got to be too much for Grandpa to keep up—particularly with his bad back. My mom stops by nearly every day and brings him groceries or dinner, but the rest of the family sees him only about once a week. I hardly ever spend time alone with Grandpa, so I felt a little funny about just dropping in on my way home from school the next day.

But Grandpa grinned his huge grin as soon as he saw me. He's missing a tooth from where a horse kicked him one time, so his grin always makes me smile back. He was sitting, as always, on his old wicker rocker on the front porch, drinking iced tea and watching the street. He stood up in his kind of stooped way and pulled over another chair for me, patted it, and sat back down.

"How is it, Ty?" he asked. Grandpa can speak English, but not all that well. I think he can understand it as well as anyone, but it's a second language for him. He'd probably be happier speaking Spanish, but like I said, no one ever spoke that in our house.

"Okay, Grandpa," I said. Then there was a long pause.

"Ines is with you?" he asked, bending his neck to look toward the parking lot. Ines is my mom, his daughter-in-law.

"No, just me today. I have . . . well, I was just wondering about something."

Grandpa looked at me and nodded.

"See, we were reading in school about the *braceros* back in the forties and fifties, and then I began wondering . . . Was that what you were—a *bracero*?"

Grandpa's smile kind of faded, and he got an almost sad look on his face. Then he looked right at me and said, "It has been a long time since I hear '*bracero*.' But, yes, Ty. That was what I was."

Grandpa stood up slowly and went into his apartment. When he returned, he was carrying two glasses of tea, and the short handle hoe was tucked under his arm. Then he sat down and told me his story.

In 1942, Grandpa was twelve years old. He lived in very poor conditions with his mother and three brothers in Mexico City. Their father had abandoned the family some years earlier. That same year, the United States entered World War II. Suddenly, because so many young men enlisted as soldiers, there weren't enough farmhands to work the crops. To solve this problem, the United States government created the "*Bracero* Program"—*bracero* meaning "hired hand." This program would allow Mexican men to come to the United States and work on the farms. The program promised decent wages, food, and even housing.

Right away, Grandpa's oldest brother left for the United States. Grandpa counted the days until he could leave too. He imagined the United States to be a wonderful land of luxury, riches, and opportunity. He'd heard all kinds of stories about how poor Mexicans became wealthy in California, Texas, and Arizona. In Mexico City, his clothes were ragged, and he was hungry all the time. He couldn't wait to leave. He thought living in the United States would be a dream come true.

As soon as Grandpa turned fifteen, he headed to El Paso. But when he arrived at the border, he was told he would have to wait for three days before being "processed" and given his work permit. He waited with hundreds of other men in filthy tents set up in the hot desert. They were given only bologna sandwiches and very little water during those three days. Finally, the men were taken to the processing center, sprayed with a white insecticide to "kill the Mexican fleas," given a contract to sign, and sent on their way.

Twenty men, along with Grandpa, were crammed into the back of a truck and taken to a beet farm in a Texas border town. In the middle of the night, they were led to their "housing"—torn and dirty tents with wooden bunks. Eight men had to share one tent, and dirt and sand blew in through the holes all night. Grandpa says he remembers crying that first night and trying to be quiet so none of the older men would hear him.

In the morning, Grandpa found out that food was *not* included in the deal, even though he had been told it was. Some of the other men had money to buy food from the farm store (the only store where Mexicans were allowed to shop), but Grandpa was flat broke. He had nothing to eat for nearly two days. Finally, some of the men noticed he wasn't eating, and they shared what they had with him.

"It was not like the dreams I'd had," Grandpa said, shaking his head. "It was a very bad dream instead."

Before the sun had begun to rise, Grandpa was handed a short handle hoe and sent to the beet fields to work, almost non-stop, for ten hours. Since the hoe was about a foot long, it could be used only by bending over nearly in half. By day's end, Grandpa said it felt like his back was on fire. The fire got worse and worse for a few weeks until it finally just turned into a constant ache. Before he was twenty, Grandpa's back was permanently bent.

"But we got paid every week. Sometimes nearly thirty dollars," Grandpa said with a little smile. "That seemed like so much money to me." But then his smile faded. "Other times we did not get fair pay at all. We were told, 'Go back to Mexico if you don't like it.' But I could not go back to Mexico. None of us could. There was nothing to return to."

So Grandpa put up with the hard work and poor treatment. He also put up with signs in town on the doors of restaurants, movie theaters, restrooms, and stores that said, "No Dogs or Mexicans Allowed." He put up with being ignored, being pushed aside, and being made to feel he was worthless. Although laws and attitudes would change over the years, Grandpa endured a difficult life, working as a *bracero* from 1945 until 1993. Even though he was referred to as a "farm worker" by the '70s and no longer used a short handle hoe, he still felt racism on a daily basis. He still saw that people ignored a poor Mexican man with a bent back, assuming he was stupid at best and a criminal at worst.

Grandpa got married in 1958, and when his wife, also a Mexican immigrant, gave birth to a little boy, Grandpa swore that his son's life would be different.

"No Spanish," Grandpa said, shaking his head. "We made it a rule in the house for your father. It was hard for your grandma and me. But English was it. No Spanish."

In Grandpa's mind, he believed that the less Mexican my father appeared to be, the easier his life would be. Grandpa encouraged my father to dress and act "non-Mexican," and he preferred for him to make friends outside of his race. Grandpa told me all this without the slightest bit of shame or embarrassment. In fact, he seemed kind of proud of the decision he had made. He seemed particularly happy that my father had married a Latino woman who also "didn't act too Mexican."

Then he looked at me for a long moment and said, "You turned out the right way, too." He grinned his funny grin, but, for once, I didn't really feel like grinning back.

It's been a while since I had that conversation with Grandpa. I wasn't sure how to feel about it at first, and to be honest, it still confuses me. I haven't talked to my father about it, because I don't know exactly what to say—I guess I'll know some day.

But I do know this: I don't think it's right that Grandpa ended up being ashamed of his roots because of how he was treated by ignorant people. If anything, he should be *proud* of everything he went through to make a better life for himself and his family. I think that somehow Grandpa figures that remembering where he came from and celebrating it would make him less of an American citizen. I think it would make him more of one.

Before I left Grandpa's apartment that afternoon, I asked him why he kept that short handle hoe if it only reminds him of how hard his life was during his first years in the United States. Grandpa just kind of shrugged and said, "I keep it so that I can be happy for who I am today. Those old days are gone. It reminds me to forget them."

I hope my grandpa lives to be 110. But when he dies, I want that short handle hoe. I'll put it up on *my* mantel so that I can remember something very different—who my grandfather *was* all those years ago in the "old days." That will make me happy—and proud.

Angela

Angela, a 21-year-old Puerto Rican woman, is sitting at the kitchen table in her apartment looking at pictures of herself from about four years earlier. She laughs out loud at many, swears under her breath at others, and just shakes her head at some.

"You can really tell here," she says, jabbing her finger at her face in the picture. "This is when I was doing a lot of crack. I've got that look, you know?" Angela stares a bit longer at the picture and then throws it back on the pile in disgust.

"It makes me so mad at myself when I think about those days. In some ways, it makes me mad at everything and everyone. I want someone to blame, but I know, I know . . ." Angela sighs and rolls her eyes just a little bit. "I know I'm responsible for my own actions. But sometimes it's not that simple. Sometimes there *are* other factors that lead you to wrong choices."

She returns to the pictures. She frowns at several more old pictures of herself, and then she holds one up and turns it around. In the picture, she's standing with one arm around a tough-looking young man covered in tattoos and wearing a bandanna. Her other hand is making a gang sign.

"People don't think about girls being in gangs, but I was. A real gang. I was what you call a *chola*." She sets the picture down on the table, still staring at it. Then she looks up with a sad smile.

"That's my baby's daddy there. I don't even know where he is anymore, and I don't care."

When Angela was thirteen, she came home from school one afternoon to find her parents screaming at each other. Her stepfather was threatening to hit her mother with a bat, and her mother was holding the phone in her hand, ready to call the police.

"It wasn't like a real unusual thing to see them fight—they did it all the time. Sometimes my stepfather would slap my mom around a little bit, but I'd never seen him really hurt her. So I was pretty scared to see him waving a bat around."

As the fight got louder and the threats got worse, Angela instinctively ran to her mother's side, begging her stepfather to stop. But her stepfather, who had been drinking most of the day, only grew angrier when he saw Angela trying to defend her mother. At one point, Angela reached out to her stepfather, trying to push him away while pleading with him.

"What happened next is kind of a blur, because he knocked me out. He always said that I fell over when he pushed me back, and that my head must have hit something. But I know damn well that he hit me with that bat."

When she speaks about that fight, Angela just shrugs her shoulders as though the memory doesn't really bother her that much, but clearly it does. She goes on to say that her stepfather often slapped her and her other sisters, sometimes hitting them with a belt or throwing things at them.

"But after that fight, I guess my stepfather felt . . ." Angela pauses, trying to think of the right way to put it. Finally she just shakes her head and says in an angry voice, "Well, I don't know or care what he felt. But he did some real messed up stuff after that. *Real* messed up."

Two nights after Angela's stepfather had hit her with the bat, he came into her bedroom late at night and sat on the side of her bed. He had been drinking again, and Angela could hear him sniffling as though he'd been crying. He reached down and put his arms around her, whispering, "I'm sorry, I'm sorry," over and over again.

"I thought he was just drunk and feeling bad for what he had done, so I pretended to be asleep. But then he just kept on holding me. It didn't seem right. And then he started touching me." Angela stops and takes a deep breath. "Well, you know, I don't want to go into detail. But he started doing things that no man should do to a thirteen-year-old. Things that someone who's supposed to be like your *father* sure as hell shouldn't do."

Like so many young girls who are sexually abused, Angela was afraid to tell anyone about what her stepfather had done—and continued doing—to her. And her stepfather warned her that if she breathed a word of it to anyone, he'd deny it, and she would look like a fool. Worse, he threatened to physically hurt her if she said anything at all. Angela soon became overwhelmed by fear and, bit by bit, began to feel all alone. In school, she stopped hanging out with her regular friends, and then her grades began to drop.

"I'd always liked school all right. I mean, I didn't make straight A's or anything, but it was okay. Not like anyone at home cared. I guess my mom wanted to see me stay in school, but my stepfather just made fun of it. He thought boys that stayed in school were sissies. He was always telling me that he never finished high school and he turned out just fine—which, of course, is a laugh."

By her sophomore year in high school, Angela was cutting classes and staying out of school more often than not. She made new friends—older kids who had already dropped out of school and spent their days hanging out on street corners, driving around in old cars, and getting into trouble. These were friends who didn't ask Angela questions, who didn't know she had changed, or that she was troubled.

"I was looking for something, I guess," Angela explains. "I didn't feel like I belonged in school. And I sure didn't feel like I belonged in my own home anymore. I just wanted to belong to something that wanted me. And I wanted to stop feeling afraid."

It didn't take long for Angela to find what she was looking for.

Angela's neighborhood, on the west side of Chicago, was nearly 90 percent Latino. It was a close-knit area where everyone seemed to keep an eye on everyone else. It was also an area that was home to several different gangs. The gangs marked their territories, sometimes only a few blocks, with graffiti and symbols. Gang members could be identified by how they dressed, which colors they wore, or which words they said.

"I grew up knowing that you had to show respect to the gangsters, or they could cause trouble for you. So, for example, when they walked by you, you had to at least nod or say hello. Just ignoring them could be a bad thing. A lot of people were afraid of them, but the gangbangers never seemed to be afraid of anything. I thought that was cool. That's what I wanted."

Two of Angela's new friends were older girls, Mina and Lupe, whose boyfriends were both in the same gang—a group that Angela simply refers to as "the Westsiders," rather than revealing the real name of the gang. The older girls bragged that they were considered part of the Westsiders, and they proudly showed off their tattoos of the gang's symbol. They went on to tell Angela that the only way to stay safe and to get respect was to join a gang.

"I told them that I didn't want to have to shoot people, and they laughed in my face," Angela remembers. "I thought the girls would have to do the exact same things the boys did, but I was wrong."

Mina and Lupe explained that gang girls take care of the boys. Sometimes that meant showing up at fights to cheer them on or bandaging them up when they got cut. Sometimes it meant stealing beer for the boys. Sometimes it meant having sex or even selling drugs. Lupe went on to say that they were expected to fight any outside girl who tried to invade their turf and steal their boyfriends. Then Lupe pulled down the neck of her shirt to show several long, ragged scars.

"Some girl she had picked a fight with had a razor taped to a chain she was wearing. Once the fight got going, this other girl just peeled off the razor and cut Lupe up pretty bad."

The thrill of the danger was appealing to Angela. But what really drew Angela in was when Mina and Lupe told Angela that the gang is a family. As long as Angela was a Westsider, she'd never have to be afraid of anything. All the other members would protect her. Anyone who messed with Angela would have to pay through pain. "A gangster has no fear," Mina told her proudly.

"Those were the two things I guess I wanted more than anything during that time in my life—I wanted to be protected, and I didn't want to be afraid anymore," Angela says sadly. "And to be honest, even though I didn't want to shoot anyone, the thought of punching someone made me feel kind of good. I was so angry at everything."

But being invited to join a gang took time. Angela would have to prove herself worthy of being a member first. And so Angela began hanging out at the abandoned garage that the Westsiders used as their base. The garage had some old sofas and chairs in it, and someone usually brought a boom box for music. The gang members sat around drinking, talking, getting and giving tattoos, and making plans.

"I learned right away that ninety percent of the time, the gangsters are just sitting around doing nothing. People always think that gangs are these horrible groups that spend all their time fighting and messing things up. But it's really not like that. To tell you the truth, everyone's just bored with nothing to do most of the time. That's why they get so excited when something finally happens."

Even so, Angela was put to the test. She went along with Mina and Lupe and stole cigarettes and beer. She took money out of her mother's purse and brought it back to the gang. She spent nights roaming the streets and days sleeping in the garage. She had sex with several of the gang members and had the gang symbol tattooed on three different places on her body. In time, she stopped going to school altogether and then dropped out during her junior year.

"I thought school was a waste of time. I hadn't thought that way before I got involved with the Westsiders, but now I was like, 'What good is geometry or English gonna do me? Nobody cares about that stuff in the real world.'" Angela sits and thinks about this for a minute and then says, "I didn't know a thing about the real world. If I had, I would've stayed in school."

Back home, Angela's mother was worried about her daughter's new and strange behavior. She tried talking to Angela, but Angela just ignored her. She tried punishing her, but Angela didn't seem to care. Meanwhile, Angela's stepfather was becoming worried too—but for an entirely different reason. Angela seemed too angry and rebellious. She stood up to her stepfather and warned him not to touch her. Her stepfather began worrying that she would, in fact, tell someone about what he had been doing to her.

"So he did what he thought he needed to do to save his own butt—he kicked me out of the house," Angela says with a bitter laugh. "In most Latino families, whatever the father says is the law. And even though he wasn't my real father, he got to make the rules. So he made up some sorry story about how kicking me out would teach me a lesson or something. My mom, like always, had no say in the matter. I told her not to worry because I had a great place to stay and a lot of friends who would help me. But I know she was worried. She made me promise to call her every day, but I hardly ever did."

Angela moved in with Mina and Lupe, who shared a small apartment with two other friends. In this "great place," Angela slept on pillows on the floor and kept all of her belongings in an old cardboard box in the corner. Cockroaches scurried around her as she tried to sleep, and more often than not, the older girls stayed up most of the night partying or arguing. Only one of the girls had a job, working three nights a week at a convenience store a few blocks away. But after stealing too many cartons of cigarettes and lifting twenty-dollar bills from the register, she was fired. Angela remembers wondering how rent got paid and how food was always in the refrigerator if no one worked. It wasn't long before Angela found out.

"Mina sat me down one night and explained how things worked," Angela says. "It was simple enough—they sold drugs, mostly crack. And now they wanted me to help them. It was like the last test. If I had said 'no,' they would've kicked me out of the apartment. And worse, I'd be on the bad side of the Westsiders. So, you see, I couldn't say 'no.'"

Angela describes that time in her life as being like a bad dream she was watching, but was powerless to wake up from. She couldn't go back home, and the relative security and structure of school was becoming just a vague memory. She had long fallen out of contact with the old friends who really *did* care about her. The fear that she thought she would lose by becoming part of a gang never disappeared. Instead, the same old fear of having nowhere to turn and no power to make her own decisions remained the same even though the setting was different. One night, she took a chance and told Mina how she felt.

"Mina seemed real understanding and didn't laugh at me or get angry. But then she kind of put her arm around my shoulder and said, 'Girl, I know what you need.' She showed me how to smoke crack, and that's a night I'll never forget and always regret. It made me feel powerful and, for once, fearless. But that feeling lasted for only a little while. Then I wanted more. And then more. As it turned out, I became an addict for nearly two years. Crack is that addictive; you think you're just going to try it once, and the next thing you know, you're stuck. And you know what? I was never powerful or fearless that whole time. I was pathetic, a loser."

Angela was being dragged down into the horrible cycle of needing to sell drugs to pay for her own addiction. As this cycle continued, she became more and more involved with the gang, needing them for protection and connections. She began a relationship with one in particular, "Gene," whose drug of choice was meth and who was one of the more violent gang members. Gene felt that Latino gangs needed to show their power by attacking whites and African Americans—and not necessarily other gang members, but simply innocent people walking down the street. He showed Angela how to load a gun and how to aim. He spent long hours preaching racial hatred to Angela, convincing her that whites and blacks were the enemy.

Angela continued to spin further and further out of control. And then one summer evening, everything came to a halt.

"There I was. Not yet eighteen years old, addicted to crack, and *pregnant!*" Angela puts her hands over her eyes as though the memory is too much. "I looked at the home pregnancy test results and felt like someone had knocked the wind out of me. When I told Gene, he was as mad as I'd ever seen him. I thought he was gonna shoot *me*. He was totally high when I told him, and the first thing he did was to aim his gun at me. And that was it. The End. I just thought, *Something has to change. Now*."

Angela remembered hearing about a place that helped girls in her position. It was known as The Safe Place, and it focused on helping young women and girls who had drug addictions and had nowhere else to turn. With shaking hands, Angela called.

"It was the first time I had made the right decision in years," Angela remembers. "I don't like to think of where I'd be today if I hadn't made that call."

Kicking her crack habit was extremely hard for Angela. She went through terrible anxiety, anger, and depression; but she was determined, for the life of her unborn son, to stay clean. The counselors at The Safe Place worked with her and made sure she was not tempted to go back to her old ways. In particular, an African American counselor named Megan talked to Angela and helped her through her toughest days.

"I always say Megan saved both my life and my son's. I remember crying and telling her about what Gene used to say about black people and how I began believing him. I was so ashamed, but Megan didn't seem to care. She explained that that's how drugs mess up your thinking."

After Angela's son, Marcus, was born, Angela remained at The Safe Place until she could get back on her feet. Although she says she never wants to see her stepfather again, she sees her mother and sisters every week now.

"I'm still angry and confused about what my stepfather did and how my mom just let him kick me out of the house. But I don't want to lose my mother. Someday, maybe, I'll tell her about what he did. I don't know. Maybe I should just let the past die in the past," Angela says quietly.

The Safe Place also helped Angela find a job. But since she had barely finished the tenth grade, the only places that would hire her were low-paying fast-food restaurants or retail shops. Angela became frustrated and bored with those jobs after a year or so. It didn't take long for her to decide to work toward her GED and finally earn her high-school diploma.

"So here I am—21 years old and still in high school!" Angela says with a laugh. "But it's all good. Once I get my GED, I'm going to look into taking some courses at the community college. And who knows after that? I'd love to be a counselor some day like Megan. There's a real need for Latino counselors."

As Angela finishes sifting through old pictures,

she goes back to one of her standing with a group of Westsiders. She stares at it thoughtfully for a while without any more anger or judgment. Finally she says, "You know, I remember hearing one time that a gangster has no fear and no goal. That's why he always stays in the same place—he won't move away from the things he should be afraid of, and he won't move toward the future. He's just stuck."

Angela puts the pictures away as her three-year-old son comes running into the room. As she settles him on her lap, she says, "But that's not me. Not anymore. I've got a past I keep moving further away from and a goal that keeps getting closer."

Diego

"I *just knew*. I knew I didn't want to mess up my life. So, I stopped hanging out with that group of kids."

Eighteen-year-old Diego Liriano is thinking back to a time that, in years, was not that long ago. But in experience, it seems like a lifetime ago. As a ten-year-old in West New York, New Jersey, just across the Hudson River from Manhattan, Diego remembers a lot of what he calls "little street gangs." These were groups of young boys, not much older than 10 or 12, who were just beginning to test their ability to get into trouble. Diego began roaming around with some of these boys when he was 10.

"I guess I was out on the street by the time I was 10. So I got sort of involved with one of those little gangs. They were mostly just doing small things like stealing cheap stuff, ringing doorbells and then taking off, getting into fights," Diego says with a slight shrug. "Not a big deal. But, still, I knew even at that age that I didn't want to be wasting my time that way."

And so by the 7th and 8th grades, Diego was making straight A's in school. Even so, he admits that he didn't study that much or regularly do his homework.

"I guess it's a good thing I'm smart," Diego says with a wide grin. "It was easy for me to remember what I heard in the classroom—easier for me than for other students. I picked things up quickly."

But Diego's teachers were confused by him. On the one hand, he did well on tests, but on the other hand he was not exactly a model student. More than once, he got suspended from school. As a result, his teachers accused him of cheating, often hovering nearby and watching him when he took tests.

"Yeah, they didn't believe I was really making the grades I was making since I'd gotten suspended. I used to cut classes now and then. I'd cut them to be with girls," he says sheepishly. "And I also got into fights. It was hard not to fight at that school; it was pretty rough."

And on the streets of West New York, in Diego's neighborhood, things were growing even rougher. As Diego describes it, no one smiled as they walked by. Rival gangs, named after the streets they lived on, passed one another without making eye contact.

"Sometimes, I'd just turn around and go the other direction if I saw someone coming my way that I didn't want to meet," Diego explains. "It was pretty bad in my neighborhood, not a very happy place."

Diego's parents, Diego Sr. and Juana, took a look around and decided it was time to move elsewhere for the sake of their children. Diego Sr. and Juana knew all too well about life being difficult when they were children. Born in the Dominican Republic into poverty, both Juana and Diego Sr. were forced to work hard jobs at very young ages. Juana worked cleaning the homes of wealthy people and sometimes made only five dollars a week. Diego Sr., hardly out of grade school, took whatever work he could find.

"They lived in homes with no electricity," Diego says. "Their bathrooms were just holes in the ground. If they ever had any books, they were hand-me-downs."

When Juana became pregnant, she and Diego Sr. made the decision to move to the United States in hopes of giving a better life and more opportunity to their child—or, rather, *children*.

"My mom didn't know she was pregnant with both me *and* my sister," Diego says with a smile. "But she began to suspect it when she started getting so big."

Diego Sr. was barely 18 when he ended up in New Jersey. He worked stocking shelves in a K-Mart, while Juana continued working and living in the Dominican Republic for a number of years before coming to the United States. In time, Diego Sr.'s mother also moved to New Jersey from the Dominican Republic in order to help with Diego, his twin sister, Diana, and later, their younger sister, Jennifer.

"All of us lived in a small apartment. I had to share a bedroom with my two sisters." Diego thinks about this for a moment. "We'd get into fights sometimes just like any brothers and sisters do, but I love my sisters very much. We're all very close." Diego says this with a fierceness, his dark eyes suddenly very serious. Then, as quickly, he laughs.

"To tell you the truth, I just kind of floated around the apartment, sleeping wherever I could—sometimes on the couch, sometimes on the floor. It was all right."

It may have been "all right," but, as Diego will often repeat, his parents were always determined to do everything they could to make sure that their children were headed along the right path, a path that would ultimately lead to more prosperous lives than what they had known. And when Diego was about 14, his parents decided to make that move from West New York, to New Jersey, to Reading, Pennsylvania. Reading, a city about an hour northwest of Philadelphia, has a high percentage of Hispanic residents with recent studies estimating the population to be roughly 51 percent Hispanic.

When Diego walked down the streets of this new town, he found that people would often smile and say hello. It seemed to be a brighter, more promising place for the family to settle.

However, one dark cloud followed the family from West New York to Reading.

"My father suffers from schizophrenia," Diego says matter-of-factly with no drama or self-pity in his voice. "It's a pretty rare disease of the brain, and no one really knows what causes it. But people who are schizophrenic, like my father, sometimes hear voices that other people don't hear. Sometimes these voices tell them to do things, dangerous things. Also, people with this disease become paranoid and believe that others are somehow broadcasting their thoughts to the world. They become convinced that others, even family members, are plotting to harm them."

Thankfully, even though there is no cure for schizophrenia, there are medicines that can treat it and make nearly all of these dangerous symptoms disappear.

"But you have to *take* the drugs," Diego says, shaking his long, curly hair. "And that was my dad's problem. He would become stubborn and believe that he had overcome his schizophrenia all on his own which, of course, is impossible. He was macho, and he'd resent anyone constantly watching him to make sure that he'd take his medication. And he'd complain that he didn't like the way the medicine made him feel."

And, so, Diego's father would stop taking his medication. Within a couple days, his behavior would change dramatically, and, on occasion, he would have what is called an "episode." When this happened, Diego says his father would become a completely different person. His face would change, and his voice would become very loud. And a few times during an episode, Diego's father tried to take his own life and, once, the life of his mother.

"He'd become religious, shouting 'It's my time to go!'" Diego recalls. "He had maybe ten episodes as I was growing up. It was always terribly frightening to me and my sisters. Once, he tried to kill himself with a pair of scissors, but my mother got to him and called the police in time. Another time, he tried to strangle his own mother, but again, we called the police."

A slight darkening of anger passes over Diego's face as he adds, "And, of course, my mother always had to be real quick to explain to the police that my dad was sick, that he couldn't help what he was doing. Because, you know, they would always just *assume* that it was domestic violence or drinking or drugs or something. They'd stereotype him."

The most recent, and most frightening, episode happened in September of 2007.

"I was the last person to see him that day. We had just come back from running an errand together. We were walking up the steps to our apartment when he told me that he was going to run across the street to the store and would be right back."

Diego takes a deep breath and continues.

"Unbelievably, I let him go—alone. I had a feeling that he was not normal. It was just the slightest little change in his face, but I knew. I just *knew*. But I held that feeling in the back of my mind and didn't act on it. As it turned out, he ended up not being 'right back.'"

Diego ran through the streets of his neighborhood calling his father's name over and over again. He ran non-stop for half an hour, looking wildly down every alley and around every corner. It seemed impossible that his father had just completely disappeared into thin air. He continued to wander through the streets for a while longer, and then became despondent.

"I couldn't get over how I, knowing all about my father's case, allowed him to go across the street without me. And now he was missing. He was gone, and I felt that it was all my fault. I felt terribly guilty."

When Diego told his mother, she was so upset

that she couldn't even speak. She was completely helpless with fear and grief. Diego went to his room and lay on his bed, face up, staring at the ceiling. It seemed as though his whole world had unexpectedly crashed into a thousand pieces, and he was the cause of the crash. Diego was immobilized by his own guilt. Down the hall, he could hear his sisters and mother crying.

"Suddenly, I came to a realization," Diego says. "I knew we were all having a hard time with this, and it was obvious that kicking myself and feeling sorry for myself would not solve anything. With my father gone, I had become the man of the family, and I had to act accordingly by showing my strength—not by hiding in my room. So I assembled a search for my father. I told my uncle, who was living with us, to put together a poster. I instructed my sisters to search around parks and places not too far away from our house on foot. Along with my cousin, then, I would drive around town searching further off places. Later that night, I went with my mother to file a missing person report at the police station."

Two days passed—two long, agonizing days of wondering where Diego Sr. had disappeared to. Diego recalls this time as being about the worst in all of his eighteen years. Although he went to school on the second day his father was missing, he could barely focus on his classes; his mind was so full of worry and fear. But, finally, Diego's taking charge and his plan of action paid off. In the afternoon of the second day, Diego's sisters wandered through a nearby park searching for their father. They came across a path that was narrow and mostly hidden, but it looked as though it had been used regularly. They followed it to a bridge and then into a dark, covered area beneath the bridge.

"That's where they found my dad," Diego says. "He was asleep on an old mattress underneath the bridge. I guess he had been there the whole time. He was very weak from the lack of food and water, and he didn't put up any kind of fight. He came home peacefully with my sisters. And he's been much better about taking his medication since that episode. I think it frightened him too."

A year later, Diego has graduated from high school and is preparing to leave for college at Lehigh University in nearby Bethlehem, Pennsylvania. Leaving with him to attend the same school will be his twin sister, Diana. Although Diego did not exactly have the easiest path through childhood and then high school, he credits a couple different things for keeping him on track in spite of the various obstacles thrown his way.

"Not long after we had moved to Reading, when I was about 14, I noticed the Centro Hispano (Hispanic Center) on the intersection of 5th and Washington Streets. If I had known then how much the Centro Hispano would ultimately end up doing for me, I would have walked in and embraced every single person in the establishment," Diego says enthusiastically, his wide smile lighting up his face.

As in other key moments in his life, Diego *just knew* that walking into the Centro Hispano and checking it out would lead to good things. And it did. Among other things, the Centro provided money for Diego to attend a three-week summer cultural and learning program at Vassar College where he met people from all over the world and made one friend in particular with whom he has become very close ("We constantly call and text each other," Diego notes). And the Centro awarded Diego with a scholarship that will help with his college costs at Lehigh.

"The scholarship is really going to help because . . ." Diego pauses for a moment and then laughs out loud. "Well, let's put it this way. I bought a used car that has cost as much in repairs as it did to buy it! That ate up a lot of money that was saved for college. I should have known that things were going to go wrong with that car. I had a feeling, you know?"

Diego is interested in studying psychology at Lehigh, in part as a way to understand his father's illness and in part to, perhaps, one day help to discover a cure through research. But Diego is also interested in psychology simply because he is fascinated with how the mind works.

"I just read a book titled *Blink*. It talks about how sometimes snap decisions are better than thinking too hard about what you should or shouldn't do. Sometimes it's better to go by feeling or instinct."

And Diego should know. That thread of instinct has followed him through his entire life. At barely 10, he *just knew* he wanted a better life than street gangs and trouble. Years later, he *just knew* that he should not have let his father walk off alone. And he *just knew* that wandering into the Centro Hispano would be a good idea. He even had an instinct about his car.

Looking to the future, Diego hopes that in ten years he will be working part time in the field of psychology or medicine and still attending school part time.

"I never want to stop learning and reading," Diego says. "I definitely see me continuing that ten years from now. And . . ." Diego rolls his eyes, thinking of what else he might be doing in ten years. "Well, I hope I'm married!" he finally says with a grin.

Diego is laid-back, however, when discussing his future. When it comes to hardcore specifics and plans chiseled in stone, he kind of shrugs his shoulders. He seems to know something about how plans can suddenly change and how roads can take unexpected detours. Still, there seems to be no doubt that his future will remain bright and that success waits for him. Diego speaks confidently of his life and how it will be ten, twenty, even thirty years down the road. It will be good. He just knows.

Sofia

Sofia giggles before explaining what surprised her most upon moving to the United States from Mexico City when she was 12. She thinks a second longer and shakes her head.

"It's really stupid," she says, still holding back another giggle.

Sofia is now 24. She works as a fitness instructor during the mornings and takes classes at a community college in the afternoons.

"Okay," she finally says and rolls her eyes. "Grocery stores!" Sofia bursts out laughing at what seems a ridiculous thing to admit.

"But you have to understand what I was used to," Sofia continues after her laughter dies down. "We lived in the city and always shopped at a *Mercado*. I'd go with my mother in the mornings, and it was really crazy. I mean, it was normal to us, but anyone here would think it was crazy."

Sofia goes on to describe a typical *Mercado* as a huge market, maybe two city blocks wide, full of hundreds of little stalls that sell everything from magical potions to oranges to chicken necks. It's packed with people nearly all day long, and the noise is almost deafening.

"Every stall has its own boom-box music playing full blast, trying to get the shoppers' attention. Then, on top of that, the vendors are constantly screaming out things like 'We've got what you want!' and 'Stop! Take a look!'" Sofia thinks back for a minute and grins. "My mother says that I used to walk around with my hands over my ears sometimes."

Food shopping was a drastically different experience in the United States.

"Oh my God," Sofia says, falling into helpless laughter again. "My two brothers and I could not even go into a grocery store for the first year we lived here without cracking up at something. It's just so quiet and clean and neat. There's really soothing music playing over your head. Everything's in packages, and people always seem so serious. The *Mercado* was always so loud with lots of bright colors and everyone running all over the place. A very different experience."

But Sofia also remembers something about the *Mercado* that doesn't make her laugh.

"Whenever we went very early in the mornings, we'd have to wait out front for the big gate to open. Also, out in front on the street were all the huge garbage containers that held all the spoiled or rotten food from the day before. There were always five or six people digging through the garbage— even children. I remember seeing the same old woman there every time. She carried a sack and a knife. She'd pick out vegetables, cut out the rotten parts, and put them in her bag. I think that's how she fed herself, maybe even her family."

Even so, most of Sofia's memories of Mexico City from when she was a child are often affectionate and sentimental. She has a large extended family scattered through the city and in nearby towns. When she and her two brothers left Mexico with their parents a little over twelve years ago, Sofia was frightened and very sad.

"Of course, it was all I had ever known. I had so many cousins and friends and family. When we would all get together for holidays, there would be hundreds of us! Or, at least, that's how it seemed. Then here we were in a new country, and except for a few friends of my parents, we didn't know anyone. Suddenly, all my friends were gone. I can't explain how that feels. But it wasn't good. My two brothers are older, and even though they looked out for me, they didn't really want a twelve-year-old girl tagging along."

But Sofia made the best of it. At her new school, she met other Latino kids whose experiences were very similar to hers. It was comforting to share her worries and fears with new friends, especially as she moved into her teen years.

"Our worries were really no different than anyone else's our age—Latino or not. I was mostly worried about not fitting in, not being liked, other kids thinking I was weird because I was from a different country. But, you know, teenagers in Mexico and the United States are not much different from each other. We all like to do the same kinds of things."

Still, Sofia experienced some difficult times and endured some difficult people.

"Oh," she remembers, laughing and shaking her head, "I can laugh about it now, but back then it made me *so* upset. There was this one group of boys, white boys who were kind of like bullies. They used to walk up to me and some of the other Latino girls and ask these really long, ridiculous questions. The questions probably didn't even make much sense, but they *really* didn't make any sense to me since my English wasn't very good. Then they'd just stand there laughing when I'd get confused or angry."

The memory clearly still upsets Sofia, even though she claims it doesn't. Her jaw gets tight and her eyes cloud over.

"They were so stupid. They used to call everyone who was Latino either *Chico* or *José*—Everyone! Even the girls! They tried to pick fights with this one Latino boy all the time because they knew he wouldn't fight back. His parents were here illegally, I think, and that poor boy was convinced that his parents would get sent back to Mexico if he got in a fight. He just put up with all kinds of abuse."

Of all the things that might have been frightening or difficult, Sofia definitely feels that the biggest roadblock was not understanding English very well when she moved here. She knew enough to get by, but not enough to have a real conversation or understand what was going on around her half of the time. Luckily, she had teachers at her new school who were very patient and helpful. One teacher in particular would often spend an hour or more helping Sofia with her English after classes were over.

"And I was determined," Sofia recalls. "Those boys who made fun of me will never know it, but it was because of them that I learned English so fast."

Every few years, Sofia's family would travel to Mexico City to visit relatives and friends. The first time they returned, Sofia remembers counting the days and marking them off a calendar in anticipation of "going back home." But five or six years later, the visit was not as exciting. Sofia remembers feeling, for the first time, that she was not *going* home but, rather, *leaving* her home in the United States.

"I remember my grandparents and particularly some of my cousins who were around my age treating me differently. It was like 'Oh, here comes Sofia. She thinks she's better than us because she lives in America,' which, of course, was not true. But I guess after that much time had passed and I had gone from 12 to 18, a lot had changed about me. And, you know, I would have changed no matter where I lived. But they'd kind of stare at me, expecting me to say or do something unusual. They still do that. I guess they always will. Their only understanding of American culture is what they see on TV."

And Mexico City did not seem the same to Sofia. The crowds, the noise, the constant rush of a city of twenty million people no longer appealed to Sofia.

"Our family had moved to Tennessee, and there couldn't be two more different places in a lot of ways," Sofia explains.

It is often said that children who grow up in Mexico City do not paint the sky blue when they paint pictures. Because of the intense pollution, children grow used to thinking of the sky as a shade of yellow or grey. Sofia describes feeling the air sting her eyes and her lungs when she returned to Mexico City after being away for so long.

"I'd never realized how terribly dirty the city was until I lived somewhere else," Sofia says. "Mexico City is the third largest city in the world, so you figure it's going to have some smog or something, but there's also a lot of poverty, so that makes things worse." Sofia pauses to think and then makes a funny face, scrunching up her nose. "One thing that is the *worst* is the city's sewer system. It's old and rundown. During every rainy season, it backs up, and all the sewage just runs through the streets. Aside from being gross, it creates a lot of sickness. I guess there isn't enough money or concern to fix it."

Sofia then describes the packs of stray dogs that roam the city looking for food. It is estimated that more than three million of these starving and desperate dogs live within the Mexico City limits. More than once Sofia has seen dogs and people fighting over the same garbage.

Sofia shakes her head and sighs. "I don't want anyone to get the wrong idea. There are also wonderful and beautiful things about Mexico City. It is where I'm from, and I'm proud to be Mexican. It's just that . . ." Sofia thinks for a moment. "It's just that I wish life wasn't so hard for so many people there."

Sofia loves her job as a fitness instructor at a small gym not far from where she lives. Some day, she hopes to complete a degree in exercise physiology and become a personal trainer for professional athletes. But it is a career that seems to point out, once again, differences between her life in America and the life she might have had in Mexico.

"One of the main reasons my parents moved us here when I was young was so that we could have better lives and more opportunity. But I think they're not too sure about the opportunity I'm going after," Sofia says with a laugh. "My father doesn't say too much about it, but my mother thinks that what I do and what I want to study is something only men should do. Her biggest concern is that no man will want to marry a woman who works in a gym."

Sofia rolls her eyes again and smiles. "I try to remember that my mother grew up in Mexico, where attitudes toward women are often very different than they are in the United States. But sometimes I think both my parents would be happier if I were married and had no career plans at all. It's frustrating for me that they feel that way. I know I'll get married some day, but I want to make something of myself and my life too. I want to do that for *me*."

Of her circle of female friends back in high school, Sofia points out that three out of six of them became pregnant while still in school. Ultimately, all three dropped out to take care of their babies as single mothers. Sofia looks sad when she talks about the high rates of teen pregnancy among Latino girls. Today, three out of five Latino girls become pregnant before the age of twenty, forcing many of them to drop out of school or give up any plans for the future.

"Probably a lot of those girls aren't getting very much support at home to have a real career or to continue on in school. It's the difference in cultures. But the way I see it is that you're here now. You have all these opportunities to make something of your life, so you ought to take them. It's not like you're putting down the culture you came from or doing something bad just because you want something better for yourself. Girls should understand that they're just as entitled to that as boys."

After living more than half her life in the United States, Sofia thinks back on all the adjusting she had to do and all the differences, big and small, that she had to get used to. When asked if there's anything she just has never gotten used to, Sofia is quick to shake her head no. But then she seems to suddenly change her mind. She giggles much in the same way she did when remembering how strange grocery stores used to seem to her.

"Okay, this is really ridiculous, but . . ." Sofia bursts out laughing and can barely get the words out. "Possums! I'm terrified of possums! I'd never seen anything as ugly as that animal when we lived in Mexico. But there are a *lot* of possums in Tennessee. It freaks me out. Still."

After laughing about this for several minutes, Sofia wipes her eyes and says, "Well, I made it through leaving all my friends, a language change, being teased, relatives who don't understand me, and a big culture change. I guess I can still be afraid of possums."

Carlos, Deena, and Luis

In 2005, nearly twenty-five percent of all Latino high school students dropped out of school before receiving their diplomas. That's a number that is nearly three times the national average, and it's a number that's alarmingly high. As you will see in the following personal stories, students drop out for different reasons. Some claim that school is too boring. Others don't like their teachers. Still others get caught up in drugs and gangs.

While there may be many different reasons for dropping out, most dropouts tend to agree on one point: high school is a big waste of time. However, nothing could be further from the truth. Studies prove that a person with a high-school diploma typically earns $10,000 more a year than a dropout earns. Further, a high-school diploma is necessary

*for college, and college graduates earn even more—
$18,000 more a year for a two-year college degree
and nearly $30,000 more a year for someone with
a bachelor's degree.*

*But there is, of course, a greater reward than
money. All high-school or college graduates know
the sense of pride and accomplishment that comes
from achieving a difficult goal. They know that
they can depend upon themselves to create their own
futures. Certainly, that is the greatest reward of
all.*

Carlos

I don't see the point. I know everyone always
says that it's important to stay in school, but they
don't know *me*. They don't know where *I'm*
coming from or anything about the life I've lived.
What's right for someone else might not be right
for me, you know? Plus, nobody in my family
ever graduated from high school except my older
sister, and what good did it do her? None that I
can see. She's earning six dollars an hour working
a drive-through window at McDonald's. She says
she's saving up for college—a big waste of time
and money, if you ask me.

My mother moved to the United States from
Mexico with her parents back in the eighties.
Grandma and Grandpa never even went to high
school at all, and they own their own home now.
My mother dropped out her senior year when

she got pregnant with my sister, and she still lives in a small apartment and works a crappy job. So like I said, what good does it do? Nearly four years of high school, and she's worse off than her own parents who barely finished the fifth grade. I can't see where education makes any difference at all.

Anyway, I'm not cut out for school. It was okay really early on, like when I was 7 or 8. I was pretty good at math and art, but there's something wrong with me that makes it hard to read, so I always hated that. We'd have to read out loud in class, and the other kids would laugh when I couldn't figure out even simple words. Then the teachers put me in a special education class when I was 10, which was even worse, because then everyone thinks you're retarded or something. I got sick of being called names, so I learned how to fight. I used to pick up pretty big rocks on the way to school and keep them in my pockets until recess. Then I'd throw them at the kids who laughed at me. So I guess you could say that it was around sixth grade when I knew school wasn't for me.

It was also around that time that I was beginning to get pretty angry about not knowing my father. I've never even met him. To tell you the truth, I don't know if my mother even knows who my father is. My sister has a different father, who lives out in California now, but at least she knows who he is, and sometimes he even sends her birthday presents and pictures of himself. Well, I just started wanting to know who my dad is. I wasn't like a crybaby about it. I was just angry.

So then I started hanging out with some of the neighborhood kids—older kids—when I started junior high. We had a little group we called the "North B's" because we used to meet on the corner of North and B streets. We weren't like a real gang or anything. It was mostly Latino guys from our neighborhood, but there were a couple of white guys, too, who used to show up now and then. We'd all go over to someone's house and drink beer and play video games or something. So, yeah, I started drinking when I was 12. I'll be honest—I didn't like the taste of it at all at first. I'd ask for a Sprite instead, and they'd all make fun of me, so I drank the beer. After a while, I kind of liked the way it made me feel. Then, next thing you know, I'm drinking every day.

High school was okay at first, to tell the truth. Like when I was younger, math came pretty easy to me, and I even got an *A* in a math class once. But all the other classes seemed like a serious waste of time—particularly English. I still hated reading, and now we had to read plays and all this really old stuff that, in my opinion, was just stupid. What good does any of that do anybody? I never heard of any job that requires you to have read Shakespeare. So I just goofed around in those classes and never did any homework. Somehow they kept passing me to the next year anyway. I'd usually get the lowest grade possible for passing. They just gave it to me even though I was failing.

By the end of my sophomore year, I was hanging with the North B's a lot more. Most of the guys had either already dropped out or were planning to. It was just so much easier to meet up with friends and have a beer and play games than to go home and do homework. And it wasn't like my mom really cared. She was having a whole lot of problems with a boyfriend and with her job. It's funny because she's always talking about going back to get her GED so that she can get a better job, but she doesn't seem to care about me graduating from high school. Sometimes she'll get on me for cutting classes, but I think that's just because she doesn't want me getting in trouble around the neighborhood. Mostly, I think she's worried she might have to pay a fine or take time off of work.

So now I'm a junior, and I'm seriously considering dropping out. I see my friends earning money while I'm wasting days sitting in boring classes where I don't learn anything that's ever going to help me. And there's another thing—I don't ever see any Latino doctors and lawyers. Know what I mean? We're always the ones cutting grass or cleaning houses or working in Mexican restaurants or something. I'm not saying that that's the way it *should* be, but that's the way it is. And I'm also not saying that I want to do that kind of work. I'll bet I can find something better. My grandpa has worked on a car assembly line for years and years and made pretty good money, so I'm sure I could do the same.

But the funny thing is that Grandpa's the only one who tells me over and over again to stay in school. He always says, "You don't want the life I have. You could do so much more." I don't get why he says that. When I ask him, "Do so much more? Like what?" he just tells me that I'll have to stay in school to find out. What kind of answer is that? Like I said—I just don't see the point.

Deena

I've got no one to blame but me. I'll just say that right up front. I talk to other girls my age who have dropped out, and practically all of them come from some pretty rough backgrounds. But me? I've got no excuse except that I made some really bad choices. I thought I knew it all and didn't need to stay in school. Then one thing led to another, and here I am—still in rehab and struggling just to get my GED.

My mother is Puerto Rican, and my father is Mexican from Sonora. But both of them grew up in the United States, and both of them are educated and work in careers that they like. My mother is a pre-school teacher, and my father works in a bank in the loan department. My whole life, they've always told me and my older sister that we can be anything we want as long as we work hard and stay on track. Well, I guess you could say that I went off track—*way* off track.

I was always very shy in school. Teachers used to send my parents notes and call them up to tell them that I was too quiet. Sometimes my grades would even be lowered because I wouldn't ever talk in class. My older sister, Jessica, was just the opposite. She was always real outgoing, laughing, and totally popular. Because I'm only two grades behind her, all the teachers assumed I'd be the same way, but I'm not. I remember my parents sitting me down, a few times, and asking me if something was wrong. Then they'd always tell me that I didn't need to feel shy just because I was Latino in a mostly white school. It's crazy because I'd never really thought about that until they pointed it out. Then it just made me more shy!

But grade school went pretty well anyway. I always loved to keep a diary ever since I had learned how to write, so writing was something I was really good at. I figure I liked it because it was a way I could express myself without having to talk. But then, around seventh grade, I had a teacher that just seemed to hate me. She would pick on me in class all the time and point out to everyone that I was shy. Sometimes I wondered if she did that because I was Latino. I never saw her being mean like that to any of the other students. So I began cutting the class and hanging out in the girls' bathroom during that hour. Some of what were considered the "bad" girls also cut classes and hung out in the bathroom smoking. Before long, I got to know them pretty well and became friends with them.

That same teacher threatened to fail me unless I did a fifteen-minute presentation in front of the class. She picked the one thing that she knew would scare me the most, so I stopped going to that class altogether. Then my parents were called, and it became a really big deal. My mother actually cried, and my father grounded me and took away some of my weekend privileges, like going to the mall and watching TV. I look at that class and that teacher as the turning point. I hated school after that.

That group of girls I met while cutting class became my closest friends. By the time I was a sophomore in high school, all I cared about was getting through the day and hanging out with them. Some of them smoked weed between classes out in the parking lot. I didn't like the way it made me feel, so I never got into that. But then one Friday night when we were all over at one of the girl's houses, someone pulled out some speed or crystal meth. I still don't know which it was, but I really liked it. It made me feel brave and not shy anymore. Suddenly, I felt like

I could talk to anyone about anything. The only problem was that when it began to wear off, I felt twice as nervous and worried. So then I had to have more. That's how addiction happens. I'd buy meth if I had enough money, but mostly I did speed because it was cheap.

Somehow, I kept my secret from my parents for a while. I think they just thought I was a little more talkative and nervous than usual— something that they may have seen as normal in a teenage girl. But before long I needed more money, and I began to get it any way I could. I worked after school and on weekends at a Burger King, but twenty hours of minimum wage wasn't cutting it. So I stole money from the register. My manager figured that out pretty fast and fired me. He couldn't prove that I was stealing money, so he didn't press any charges. But he kicked me out of there.

So you can probably guess what happened next. Some of the girls I hung around with sold drugs, and when I complained about getting fired, they said, "Why waste your time working like that? You can make a hundred times that selling." So midway through my junior year, I began selling meth. Just a little here and there at first. But then the money became addictive too. I started cutting classes more and more so that I could sell. I figured I was making more money than I'd ever make by staying in school. I thought I had it all figured out. Everyone else was stupid, and I knew the real road to success. Yeah, right.

I'm lucky that I have the parents I have. Believe me, I didn't feel that way at the time, but I do now. My mom finally sat me down and refused to leave my room until I told her what was going on. I wouldn't say a word. So she and my dad just began going through everything in my room—drawer by drawer, under my bed, everything. They found both drugs and money. I tried to make up some lame story about how it wasn't mine, but of course they knew it was.

So I've been in rehab on and off for about a year now. I think I've finally kicked the drugs, but it's been extremely difficult. And obviously I had to drop out of school to get clean and put my life back together. I'm studying for the GED, but after cutting so many classes, going to classes high, and not caring for so long, it's kind of tough. I have to remind myself over and over again that finishing school is for the best. It's been a long time since I've believed that's true. Old habits are hard to break in more ways than one.

Sometimes I think back to that teacher in the seventh grade and wonder if my life would have been different if she hadn't treated me the way she did. But then I guess there will always be some bad teachers or people who will try to lead you the wrong way. In the end, the way your life will go is up to you. It's taken me nineteen years to figure that out.

Luis

My story is really common, and the fact that it's so common is pretty sad, I think. When I was younger, I used all sorts of excuses for why I wanted to drop out of high school. Everyone's heard them: the classes were boring, the teachers were no good, I wanted to make money, graduating from high school wouldn't help me in the real world, and so on. But probably the main reason I ended up dropping out was because I couldn't speak or write English very well at all, and I was too stubborn to ask for help. Or maybe I was just too lazy to take the help that was offered. Either way, it really affected my life for a number of years.

I moved here from Mexico with my family when I was 14. That's a real awkward and difficult time for a boy to move to another culture. I have two younger sisters and an older brother. He was nearly 18 when we moved here, so I don't think it was as difficult for him. He never went to school in the United States; he just began working. I remember being jealous when he would head off to a job every morning to earn money, and I had to go to school. I asked my parents about a hundred times if I could just work too, but of course they told me no. I was still just a kid.

School was different here than in Mexico. It was the same in that we went to classes, had homework, and took tests, but it was different in other ways. Things were a lot more strict and moved a lot more quickly. For example, we used to have fifteen minutes between classes in Mexico. During that time, you could do whatever you wanted—go outside, get something to eat, whatever. But here, there are only a few minutes between classes. Also, in Mexico we always went home for lunch and got plenty of time for it. Here, we had to eat in a cafeteria or lunch room with everyone else. That was where things were first really hard for me.

There were some other Latino kids in my freshman class, but not many. The few that were there kept to themselves and didn't seem to want to make a point of meeting me. It was almost like they didn't want to draw attention to the fact that they were Latino by becoming friends with someone else Latino. It sounds crazy, but that's how they acted. I made the mistake, just once, of saying something in Spanish to one of them and getting totally ignored.

I could make it through classes without feeling too out of place. I mostly would hide in the back of the class and keep my head down. Honestly, I couldn't understand a lot of what the teachers were saying anyway. But lunchtime was hard. That's where you're kind of on display if you're sitting alone, if no one speaks to you. Right away, I felt like a loser and like I didn't belong in that school. It only got worse when, finally, a couple guys sat across from me and tried to strike up a conversation about a class all three of us were in. I was so nervous about my English that I just sort of dissed them. After that, no one talked to me.

Somehow, I got passed in all my classes to my sophomore year. I don't know how. I don't think I could read or write English much better than an eight-year-old by the end of my freshman year, but I got passed. Honestly, I think some of the teachers just didn't care. They didn't want to see me in their classes again, hiding and not participating. But there were a couple teachers who really tried to help. My English teacher, Mrs. McLeod, always asked me to stop by her classroom when I got a chance so that she could explain the marks on my papers and help me with some of the language stuff. I always told her I would, but I never did. I was angry and embarrassed about my poor English skills. I sure didn't want to sit down and try to talk about it to an *English* teacher!

I was never a troubled kid. By that, I mean I never got into drugs, drinking, or gangs. I just didn't want to be in school. I wanted to earn money so that I could buy a car—a sports car. I'd lie awake at night thinking about how I'd get a good job, buy my car, and then cruise by the high school when it was letting out so that everyone could see me. *That* would show them! The little Mexican kid that everyone ignored, already earning money and driving around in a fancy car.

I became obsessed with the idea of it. I began cutting classes near the end of my sophomore year. One month into my junior year, I dropped out. My parents were disappointed, but they didn't force me to go back. After all, neither of them had a high-school diploma. What could they say?

I found out right away that there were no "good jobs" for high-school dropouts. Nearly every job application asked where I had graduated from high school. I finally settled for being a busboy at a restaurant two blocks from our house. It paid minimum wage. That wasn't nearly enough to buy a car, so I got a second job working at a bakery from midnight to eight in the morning. I cleaned the machinery in the bakery and swept the floors. Because I had no diploma and couldn't speak English very well, they wouldn't give me any other position, even though there were better-paying positions available. I was exhausted all the time, but I finally saved enough to get a decent car.

But I discovered a funny thing when I got my car. It didn't really make me feel any better about myself. In my heart, I knew I could be more than a dish washer and a floor sweeper. Still, I was too stubborn and embarrassed to ask for help. As a result, I continued to work in these boring, low-paying jobs for nearly two more years. Then one night at the restaurant, something happened that was a turning point for me.

As I was clearing off a table, I overheard a

couple speaking in Spanish at a table nearby. They were discussing the menu and trying to figure out how to order. Clearly, they knew no English at all. A new waitress, who was nervous and kind of short-tempered, waited on them. I could hear her getting more and more frustrated with their inability to speak English. Finally, she refused to serve them and basically told them to leave and not come back until they could order in English. The Latino woman looked as though she might cry, and her husband hung his head. More than anything, I wanted to help them, but I wasn't sure if *my* poor English would only make things worse. I guess I'd never felt so frustrated and angry. At that moment, I knew what I had to do.

That was four years ago. Since then, I've taken classes to improve my English, both speaking and writing. After that, I took the GED exam and passed pretty easily. After all, I'm not stupid—I just hadn't learned a language that I needed to learn. I have a lot of big plans now—a lot bigger than buying a car. I'd like to learn how to work as a translator and maybe a teacher for new immigrants. I'd also like to visit high schools and tell my story to Latino students who may be thinking of dropping out for the very same reason. I know firsthand how hard it can be to struggle with English, but there are a lot of people out there who are willing and able to help. I'd like to become one of those people now.

Arelys and Dr. Q

*S*ometimes it may seem as though everything is against us when we have a dream that we're pursuing. This can be especially true when it comes to education. Often, all sorts of roadblocks seem to get thrown in our way—not enough money, not enough time, no support from friends or family. Still, we push on, knowing that all the work and worry will be worth it in the end. The following stories present two Latino people who overcame unbelievable odds to realize their dreams of better lives through education.

Arelys

Arelys Sanchez remembers spending most of her early childhood years being constantly shuttled back and forth between her mother's apartment in the Bronx in New York City and her relatives' homes in Puerto Rico. Her mother was a single parent and had little money and even less promise for a better future. So, when things got too difficult for her mother, Arelys and her brother were sent to stay with relatives who could take care of them until life became more stable back in New York.

When Arelys reached school age, her mother's situation improved enough for Arelys to remain with her mother full time. But life in the Bronx was anything but peaceful.

"My neighborhood was very dangerous," Arelys remembers. "And even in grade school, I was exposed to drugs. There were fights in my school every day—all the time. If my mother wasn't there to pick me and my brother up right away after school, it could be very bad for us. And even when she was there, we still got slapped around on our way to the car."

Arelys's mother worked constantly to support her two children. But without much more than a grade-school education, her mother could not find jobs that paid enough to feed and clothe three people. Washing dishes, scrubbing floors, and doing other people's laundry, sometimes for ten or twelve hours a day, was hard and constant work, but it was not enough.

Arelys would often hear her mother crying in her small room down the hall at the end of a long day. Hearing her mother cry caused unbearable pain for Arelys, so she finally made up her mind to do something about it.

"Eighth grade was my last year of education," she says with a small laugh. "I dropped out of school so that I could help support my mother and my younger brother. I *had* to."

Arelys, barely thirteen, walked into the hiring offices of J.C. Penney feeling, as she recalls, "scared as heck." She was given a simple job, and the added income eased the problems at home for a while. However, Arelys quickly grew bored and restless with the day-after-day routine of working eight hours at an uninspiring job and then coming home at night to her mother and brother. As a result, she channeled her energy into becoming more and more serious with her boyfriend. At fifteen years old, she was married. One year later, she had her first child.

But it didn't take very long for Arelys to discover her young husband's "rules" for her.

"It was fine for me to work and bring home the money, but I wasn't supposed to do anything else," Arelys says with a defiant toss of her head. "I suppose that's what triggered my desire to go out and get my GED."

Although Arelys had been out of school for a while, she passed her GED exam with honors. Her score was high enough to help place her in a job with the New York Housing Authority. At the time, the Housing Authority desperately needed Latino employees to communicate with and assist Latino residents.

"And so all the Latinos who came into the office were sent to me," Arelys says. "But after I was there for a while, I noticed that even though the Housing Authority really needed me, I wasn't paid nearly as much as the other employees, and I never got a promotion. I was angry at first, and then I figured out why this was happening—I didn't have a college degree. I always knew that education was important, but that was the first time I saw firsthand just how important."

Wasting no time, Arelys began taking classes at Bronx Community College. Because the Housing Authority job was fulltime and many of the classes Arelys needed took place during the day, she had to quit that job. In its place, Arelys managed to juggle four part-time jobs, often working evenings and weekends. In time, Arelys's ambition and desire to better her life took its toll on her marriage. Her husband grew jealous and suspicious of her, not understanding why she would need or want more than her family and an average job. He thought her dreams were foolish. So, instead of encouraging Arelys, he fought with her and told her she was being selfish.

But Arelys would not be discouraged. Although it was very hard on her, she divorced her husband and moved closer to her mother so that her mother could help raise her young daughter while Arelys continued her studies. But just when Arelys could almost see the light at the end of the tunnel, and her associate's degree was only a handful of classes away, tragedy struck. Her mother was diagnosed with cancer. Without a second thought, Arelys dropped out of college to take care of her mother.

It's never too late to return to school. Arelys had often heard this during the years she cared for her mother and struggled as a single mother. She kept this in mind for quite a long time—she would not be able to return to college until her daughter was a grown woman. But at 39, Arelys finally graduated from Bronx Community College with a degree in medical researching. All her hard work and dedication to a dream paid off—she was offered a scholarship to William Paterson University in New Jersey for her bachelor's degree. Once finished with that, Arelys did not want to stop. She applied to Brandeis University for graduate school. And though Brandeis is a top university and quite difficult to get into, Arelys was accepted.

"What followed were some difficult times, both financially and personally," Arelys admits. As the only Latina in her major, Arelys experienced racism and disbelief that she would be able to succeed at a school primarily attended by privileged white students. Some students also treated her rudely because she was older. Additionally, the school was exceedingly expensive, and though Arelys received more scholarships, she was always scraping money together for bills and expenses. And on top of all this, Arelys was involved in a serious car accident midway through her degree. She was injured so severely that she missed two entire semesters of classes.

But in 2007, Arelys received her Ph.D. in psychology. Today, Dr. Arelys Sanchez researches the effects of diabetes on Latino women. More than anything, she wants to give back to her own community.

"One of the problems I saw was that research always focuses on men and Caucasians," Arelys explains. "Women are not included. Latinas are not included. What I discovered was quite sad."

Arelys's research revealed that diabetes in Latino women often leads to a lessening of the ability to think and reason clearly. No one had ever known this before—it was a groundbreaking discovery that made news around the world. But for all of Arelys's amazing achievements, there is one success that stands out above the rest and brings her to tears when she speaks about it.

"My daughter grew up knowing the importance of education. That means more to me than anything else. Now I tell everybody, 'My daughter is a speech pathologist!'" Arelys says with tears in her eyes. "And then I tell everybody that I'm a grandma of three and all three say, 'We're going to college just like Grandma!' Now *that's* a dream come true."

Dr. Q

"I was nineteen years old with ten dollars in my pocket, and I didn't speak one word of English." Dr. Alfredo Quinones, or "Dr. Q," as his friends call him, remembers the night he crossed the Mexican-American border illegally. The minute he crawled over the barb wire fence in Calexico, he was caught by the U.S. Border Patrol and escorted back into Mexico.

"I waited a few hours and crossed again at the very same spot. I figured the police would not expect the same guy to cross in the same spot on the same night. I was right. Sometimes you just have to take chances."

Quinones grew up poor in the border town of Mexicali in Baja, Mexico. At only five years old, he was pumping gas and doing odd jobs to help his family. The family of seven managed to get by until 1976, when the Mexican government drastically changed the value of the peso so that it was nearly worthless. Suddenly, like millions of other Mexicans, the Quinones family lost everything.

"I remember going to the back of the house to find my father crying," Quinones, who was eight years old at the time, says. What followed were terrible years of poverty. Quinones worked at a taco stand to earn extra money, but his parents insisted that he keep up with his schooling no matter how hard times got.

"My father kept telling me, 'You want to be like me? Just never go to school.' And I was not going to follow the same path."

But it was neither an easy path nor one that seemed to pay off. Quinones attended a school many miles away. He had to get up at 4:30 every morning to take a bus, but in the afternoons there were no buses. More often than not, he had to either hitchhike or walk for hours in the desert heat to get home. This went on for years until Quinones finally graduated from high school near the top of his class. He had always wanted to be a teacher, and now he had high hopes of landing a decent teaching job, since only a high-school education was required.

But it didn't turn out that way. Because his family had no political connections and no money, Quinones was assigned to teach at a very bad school hundreds of miles away. The good teaching jobs were saved for the young men and women who came from "better" families with political connections.

"I wasn't willing to put up with that injustice," Quinones says. So, along with his cousin, he made plans to jump the border and work in the fields picking tomatoes, broccoli, corn, and grapes.

"You will spend the rest of your life working in the fields." This is what Quinones's cousin told him one afternoon as the two of them picked broccoli, their hands bleeding and the sun burning them. But Quinones would not accept that. He was determined to prove his cousin wrong.

"Not long after he said that, I started taking classes at the local community college so that I could learn English. I knew that was the first step."

Another incident that fueled Quinones's drive to succeed occurred just a few weeks after he began his classes. The son of the farmer on whose farm they were working walked by Quinones and his cousin one morning. He did not say hello; he didn't even smile. Quinones recalls that the son "looked at us like we were less than dirt." Quinones vowed to himself that he would one day get the respect he deserved. He also vowed that he would *never* treat others as though they were worth less simply because of their skin color or job.

As Quinones's English improved, so did his job. Proving his cousin wrong rather quickly, Quinones found work as a welder once he was able to speak well enough to communicate with the other workers. Now he was able to work nights and attend classes at the community college during the day. Although often exhausted, Quinones did very well. He discovered that he had a very strong talent for understanding and explaining math and science. Soon, he was tutoring students at the college in addition to working and taking classes. And so Quinones began to dream bigger—he decided that when he finished his two years at the community college, he would set his sights on an undergraduate degree at the University of California at Berkeley. But he still wasn't sure what he wanted to major in. Then, one night at work, something happened that made his path a bit clearer.

"I had an accident that caused me to reevaluate my life. I was doing a welding job on a railroad, and I fell into a tank car that was used to carry liquefied petroleum gas. It nearly killed me. By the time I was rescued, my heart rate had slowed almost to zero, but I was revived in time. When I awoke, I saw a person dressed all in white, and I was flooded with a sense of security, confidence, and protection, knowing that a doctor was taking care of me. I saw this physician at my bedside; I felt I had reached terra firma, that I had a guardian."

At Berkeley, Quinones kept the idea of being a doctor in mind, but he wasn't sure if any medical school, much less a good medical school, would accept him. However, near the end of his time at Berkeley, he met with his advisor. As his advisor looked over Quinones's transcripts and listened to Quinones express his doubts, he shook his head. Then he looked up and smiled.

"My advisor looked right at me and said that I had a very good chance of getting into *Harvard* Medical School! I thought to myself, 'This guy is clearly living *la vida loca*,'" Quinones says. "But as my advisor continued to talk, my mind raced. I thought of my grandmother, who had been a *curandera*, a town healer in the small Mexican village where I grew up. She worked mostly with herbs and natural healing. I saw the respect that she had and how much she helped people. I decided to give it a shot."

Despite his initial doubts, Quinones was accepted by Harvard. During his third year of medical school, he had the opportunity to observe brain surgery, and it had a profound effect upon him.

"I'll never forget watching the surgeons pull back the dura [the layer that separates the brain from the skull] and exposing a real, live, throbbing human brain. I recall feeling absolute awe and humility."

Today, Dr. Alfredo Quinones is one of the most highly respected and accomplished brain surgeons in the country. In the course of only ten years, he went from a penniless illegal immigrant to a graduate of Harvard Medical School. He has since become a United States citizen and married a young woman he met at his community college. Sometimes it is hard, even for Quinones, to believe he came so far so fast. But he strongly believes that with a dream *and* with education, anything is possible.

"Like many other illegal immigrants, I arrived in the United States able only to think about those dreams," Dr. Q explains. "But, now, as a citizen of the United States, I am also participating in the great journey of this country. For immigrants like me, this voyage still means the pursuit of a better life—and the opportunity to give back to society."

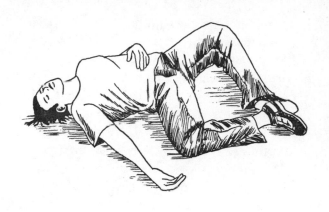

Martin

"Why did I come to the United States?" Martin Ortero sits and thinks about this question for a long moment. He has a half-smile on his face, as though he already knows the answer, but is not exactly sure how to say it. He fiddles with a pencil, sighs, and then looks up. The smile is gone.

"You know, many people in America just always assume that Mexicans come here only to earn more money and escape bad times back home. There's this idea that all Mexicans live in shacks with dirt floors or something."

Martin is an intense young man. He taps his feet constantly as he speaks, and tugs at his short beard. At 23, he has been in the United States for seven years. Now in his junior year of college, he has just recently finished applying for permanent residency.

"Obviously, not everyone comes here to escape poverty. Everyone in Mexico is not poor and uneducated, though some people seem to think that. Many Mexicans come here to escape other things—things that have nothing to do with money." Martin pauses. "I know I did," he says quietly.

Martin grew up in the city of Monterrey in northern Mexico, in the state of Nuevo León. Monterrey is the second largest city in Mexico, and it is often thought of as one of the wealthiest cities in the country, with the most educated people. It is a colorful city surrounded by the towering Sierra Madre Mountains. Many of the neighborhoods and homes in this desert city look quite similar to American homes in desert locations such as Phoenix or Albuquerque.

"Like most everyone I knew, we had a big family," Martin says. "Three boys and one girl. But unlike what people assume about Mexican families, we didn't live crammed together in a little adobe or something. We lived in a big two-story home just on the edge of the city. We had cars and nice clothes, and we went to good schools. I could speak English nearly fluently before I was 12—everyone in my family could."

Martin's father was a businessman who work-ed in the *maquiladora* industry. *Maquiladora*s are factories that put together things—electronics or car parts or even guitars—and then ship the final product to companies overseas. It is often cheaper for the companies to have the work done in Mexico, since most of the workers hired are women who will agree to work for very low wages. Many of the *maquiladora* employees, working at Mexican minimum wage, make only one-sixth of what American employees would earn at a similar job. For a full day, a worker might make six to ten dollars.

"My father is in charge of one of the *maquiladoras* that put together car stereos," Martin says, shaking his head. "He makes a lot of money, but the employees are poor. And many of the women who work there are treated badly, even getting fired if they become pregnant. The women are afraid to complain or stand up for their rights. It's not like American culture in Mexico when it comes to people's rights a lot of the time. Women are often taken advantage of, and everyone thinks it's okay."

Martin goes on to explain that he didn't really think or care about the *maquiladora* workers as he was growing up. It was just his dad's job. But then, in high school, he became friends with a girl whose mother had worked for years in one of these factories. The friendship opened his eyes and mind to a different way of looking at things. Slowly, he came to realize that he didn't agree with his father's opinions about these female workers. Martin had grown up hearing his father make belittling and sexist comments about women in general, but particularly about the employees at his *maquiladora*. In his father's opinion, the female workers were stupid, and it was their own fault if they were poor. They were next to worthless and got what they deserved. In time, Martin grew angry. Then one day, he decided to confront his father.

"He just laughed at me," Martin recalls with a frown. "*Laughed!* It was clearly not something my dad thought was even worth discussing. He's old school, you know? Very macho. So that was the first time I really disagreed with my father. But that was nothing compared to a couple years later when I was 17."

Martin pauses, thinking for a minute while tapping his feet and spinning the pencil around. He seems reluctant to start talking again. Finally, he sets the pencil down and folds his arms.

"Why did I leave Mexico? Okay. Here's what happened when I was 17." Martin looks a little worried. "I'll warn you. It's not a happy story, but it's true."

Martin was the second of three brothers. His sister was quite a bit younger than the boys, so she generally didn't spend a lot of time with them. However, the three brothers were very close. In particular, Martin looked up to his older brother, Matteo. Matteo was three years older and seemed to do well at anything he put his mind to. He was an excellent soccer player, he could rebuild engines, and he had even taught himself to play guitar well enough to perform in a neighborhood band.

"Sometimes older brothers don't want their younger brothers hanging around all the time, but Matt was different. He was always real happy to show me how he did things. I wasn't as patient with my younger brother, Enrique, so Enrique, who was five years younger, was always hanging around watching Matt too. Matt was always okay with that. Some of his friends teased him and called him *la ninera* (the nanny), but he didn't care."

When Matteo graduated from high school, he decided that he wanted to attend college in the United States—a decision that seemed strange to his parents, but they did not oppose it. Martin says his brother had begun to seem anxious and restless during his last two years in high school—traits that seemed at odds with Matteo's generally easygoing personality. By his senior year, Matteo was staying out much later than he was supposed to many nights. He'd sneak up to his room at two or three in the morning, and Martin would often hear him. Once or twice Martin tried to get his older brother to tell him where he had been, but Matteo would always shrug it off and just say "hanging out."

After graduating, Matteo decided to work a construction job for a year to save more money for college. It was a physically demanding job, and he was often too tired to go out at night, but he continued to distance himself from the family. Martin also remembers Matteo arguing with their father on more than a few occasions over things that seemed so unimportant.

"And then a lot of his old friends seemed to turn on him," Martin remembers. "It was really weird because these were guys my brother had known for years—friends from his soccer team and guys in the band. Over that summer, they started ignoring him. Then Matt got into a fight with one of them and got his nose broken. After that, a lot of those guys called him names like 'gay,' or *marica* and *afeminado* [also meaning 'gay']. They also went back to calling him *la ninera* again, something they hadn't said in years, but this time they weren't saying it jokingly. All along, I just figured it was because he had lost the fight and cried when his nose got broken. Still, I couldn't understand why they were all so mean to him like that."

But even in the midst of all this, Matteo still took time now and then to do things with his younger brother. Usually on a weekend night, Matteo and Martin would drive into town to check out the new arrivals at a used-CD-and-comic-book store. Both brothers collected old comic books, and at one time, Matteo had even shown some promise as a cartoonist. After leaving the store, they often crossed the street to get something to eat at a restaurant where a lot of the local high-school kids hung out. In the past, the brothers had often stayed at the restaurant socializing for a few hours, but now Matteo was always ready to leave as soon as they finished eating. And after the fight, Matteo often didn't want to go to the restaurant at all.

One hot Saturday night in August, Matteo and Martin headed downtown as usual. It would not be long before Matteo would be leaving for college, so Martin was particularly eager to spend as much time as possible with his brother. As they were leaving the CD-and-comic store, Martin remembers Matteo staring at the restaurant across the street with a worried expression.

"It was like he saw something or someone he didn't want to see. Since it was summer, everyone was sitting on the deck or along the sidewalk. You could see everyone who was there. I looked across the street, but nothing looked funny to me. I asked him what he was looking at, and he just said, 'Nothing. But let's go somewhere else to eat. I'm sick of that damned place.'"

Matteo and Martin got in their car. Matteo turned the key and . . . nothing. The car wouldn't start. Matteo checked under the hood and determined that it was the starter, not the battery. It was a repair that would have to wait until the next day. The brothers sat on the hood discussing what to do. As two teenage boys, neither of them wanted to call their parents to come and pick them up—not on a Saturday night and particularly not right across the street from a hangout. In the end, they decided to walk the two miles home. It was cooler now, and they would pass another restaurant on the way.

As they turned to head down the street, a loud voice shouted Matteo's name from across the street at the restaurant. Matteo just kept walking, but Martin turned around.

"It was this big guy I'd never seen. He looked older than a lot of the kids there. He yelled Matt's name again, and when Matt kept ignoring him, the guy started shouting '*Marica!*' and a bunch of other rude things at him. Then the guy yelled something like, 'Is that your boyfriend?' and pointed at me. Matt turned around then and gave the guy the finger. The guy gave it back to him and then stood up like he was going to come across the street. At that point, Matt just grabbed my arm and told me to keep walking."

As they walked, Martin asked his brother what was going on and why that guy seemed mad at him. Matteo would say only that it was a stupid misunderstanding and not a big deal. But Martin could hear his brother's voice shaking. In the streetlights, he could see a kind of fear and anger on his brother's face that he'd never seen before. They walked quickly, deciding to go straight home instead of stopping. But about a half mile from their home, in an empty area that separated the city from the neighborhood, Martin heard sudden footsteps. It sounded like running—and it sounded like more than one person.

"What happened then—" Martin stops and takes a deep breath to calm himself down. "What happened then seemed like a horrible blur. The big guy from the restaurant came running toward us, and he had two other big guys with him. One of them was carrying a pipe or a piece of metal. Two of them jumped on Matt before I could even say anything, and the other one grabbed me and kicked me in the stomach. I couldn't breathe or speak—just sprawled on the ground watching them beat Matt.

"And the whole time they kept yelling 'fag' and every other anti-gay name they could think of. I remember thinking that they had the wrong person. My brother wasn't gay. Like Matt had said, this must be a misunderstanding. And I kept thinking, *Say something, Matt! Don't just lie there! Tell them they're wrong!* Then the guy from the restaurant came over and kicked me in the head. And everything went dark. The next thing I knew, I woke up with a sharp pain in my head, and Matt was lying next to me totally still."

Martin tried to wake his brother up, but he couldn't. He checked for a pulse and thought he felt a weak one. Blood was running down Matteo's face from a dent in his forehead, and his right arm was turned at a horrible angle over his head. Pulling his older brother's cell phone out of his jacket pocket, Martin called home, crying and screaming into the phone when his mother picked up. Within minutes, his parents arrived and rushed their oldest son to the hospital. The doctors worked on Matteo for several hours in an attempt to stop the bleeding and stabilize him. But at four in the morning, he lapsed into a coma. Just before sunrise, he died.

"They never found the guys who did it." Martin stares angrily into space. "The truth is, I don't think the police tried too hard to track them down. Because when all the facts came out, it turns out that Matt *was* gay. He'd been hiding it for years because he knew what our father would do—he'd have thrown him out of the family without a second thought. Like I said, my dad was the old-school macho type. I'd heard him say a million times that 'all fags should be killed.' I know my dad was heartbroken when Matt died, but to this day, he won't speak his name. It's like his own son never even existed! I just can't . . ." Martin's voice trails off as tears come into his eyes. The pencil he's been fiddling with snaps in half.

Martin made up his mind during his senior year in high school to follow in his older brother's footsteps. In honoring his memory, he would move to the United States and go to college. Martin adds that he looks forward to becoming a citizen of the United States one day because he feels that people are given more freedom here and that differences in race, gender, and sexual orientation are respected.

"I'm realistic, though," Martin adds. "I know that people in the United States are discriminated against too at times. Even I have had some kinds of unfair treatment now and then because I'm Mexican. But things here are way ahead of Mexico. I just couldn't stay there anymore. Not after what happened."

In addition to his studies in computer science, Martin spends time doing fundraising for human rights organizations. He still returns to visit his family a couple times a year, but relations with his father are strained.

"I made the mistake of trying to talk to him a couple times about how I felt," Martin says, shaking his head. "It was just like I was 15 again and trying to talk to him about the *maquiladora*. But instead of laughing at me, he just walked away. Now, if we talk about anything, we talk about things that don't matter very much."

Martin admits that he misses Mexico, regardless of his bad memories and experiences. After all, it was his home.

"I guess, really, no one leaves Mexico to *escape*," Martin says, reconsidering his earlier words. "Mostly, we come here looking for a better life. Who can hold that against anyone? That was Matt's dream." Martin pauses and thinks for several seconds. "And now it's mine."

Yecenia

"I have a younger sister and two younger brothers," Yecenia says with a sheepish grin. "And they're *all* taller than I am!"

At only four feet, eleven inches tall, Yecenia Olmos may be small in size, but she is a towering example of what can be achieved with determination, education, and a vision of the future. It is a vision that has been constantly fueled by a desire to lead a life better than her own parents' lives—and no one has been more supportive in fueling that desire than her father.

"My father moved here from his home in Zacateras, Mexico back in the seventies because there were no jobs and no opportunities left there," Yecenia explains. "So he came to the Los

Angeles area and began working washing dishes in a barbecue restaurant. His older brothers were already here, so he stayed with them."

Yecenia pauses and adds quietly, "He only had a fourth-grade education. He was only twelve years old when he moved here."

Thirty-six years later, Yecenia's father works thirteen to sixteen hours a day as a metal grinder, still only earning minimum wage. Yecenia affectionately describes her father as stern and "grumpy" most of the time. However, she acknowledges that he is often too tired to be anything but grumpy. It has not been an easy life for a man who has had to support a family of six on minimum wage.

"He's taken a long, hard look at his own life and insisted that the life of his children be better," Yecenia says. "Since I'm the oldest child, I have had to set the example. All through school, he demanded that I make straight A's. No B's were allowed! Sometimes I felt angry and pressured, but I understood that he insisted on A's because he loved me. He wanted better things for me. *I* wanted better things for me."

And so Yecenia made nothing less than an A in every class all the way through high school. She graduated at the top of her class. A full scholarship to UCLA followed. If it all sounds too easy and like a bit of a fairy tale come true, hold on. The path to Yecenia's success was hardly a yellow brick road.

Yecenia was born and raised in South Central Los Angeles. Until she began college four years ago, South Central L.A. was the only world she had ever known. "South Central," as it is often called, has had a reputation for decades as being a hub for drugs, violence, gang activity, and poverty. It was the location of the 1992 riots that erupted after Rodney King was beaten by a group of Los Angeles police officers. And years earlier it had been the site of the 1965 Watts riots—five days of violence also resulting from police brutality. South Central is also infamous as being the home to the original Bloods and Crips gangs; gang violence mixed with drug warfare is a daily occurrence. And woven through all this is a mean thread of poverty. It is a poverty so intense that some parts of South Central have been compared to Third World countries.

This is what Yecenia knew as home. And until last year, Yecenia's only experience of the building she knew as home was a garage divided into two rooms.

"It was a garage connected to my aunt's home," Yecenia explains without a shred of self-pity or embarrassment. She smiles and simply says, "It was just really small."

All through her youth and into adulthood, Yecenia slept in the same room with all her siblings and her parents. The children slept in bunk beds pushed against the walls, and the parents slept on the floor between their children. One small closet served to store everyone's clothes, and two very small windows barely allowed any light into the converted garage. A makeshift kitchen had been built into one corner, but the bathroom was outside.

"Yes, luckily there is no snow or ice in Los Angeles," Yecenia says with a good-natured smile, recalling having to walk outside, sometimes even in the middle of the night, to use the bathroom. Perhaps worse than this, however, was never having any privacy or any space of her own. Yecenia says that it was often very frustrating to be a young girl and then a teenager whose life was constantly on display to everyone else in the family. It was the cause of fights with her siblings from time to time, but then again, it was all any of the children had ever known.

"Still," Yecenia says, "I became aware pretty quickly that other people had more room. I saw that some of my friends even had their *own* rooms. At a young age, I knew we were poor. That awareness is part of what put the drive in me to have a different kind of life some day. I knew it was possible."

But the path to that "some day" would have some twists and turns. Around 7th grade, Yecenia became involved in something that created what she now calls the biggest disappointment she has experienced so far in her young life— disappointment in herself. For a number of reasons that Yecenia can't even fully explain or understand, she became drawn to a tough gang of girls.

"It wasn't really a gang like what you picture when you think of *gangs*. I mean, it was a group of thirteen-year-old girls! Basically, it was this sisterhood of thirteen-year-old girls who wanted to prove how tough they were by fighting."

To be accepted into the group, Yecenia had to endure being beaten by the other girls. Covered with scratches and bruises, Yecenia would wear long-sleeved shirts even in warm weather so that her parents wouldn't see the marks of her involvement in this group. South Central L.A. is home to many real and dangerous gangs. Yecenia's parents were well aware of how being drawn into the gang life, regardless of how harmless at first, could destroy a young person's life. They had often spoken to their children about the mistake of throwing one's future away by joining gangs. Ultimately, it was her sorrow at the thought of letting her parents down that turned Yecenia away from the young gang.

"Plus," she reveals with a laugh, "I wasn't a very good fighter at all. It just wasn't in my nature. But more than that, I began to think about what I was doing. I realized that hanging out with these girls would not do anything to help me achieve my goals. I guess I had just felt like I wanted to belong to something—you know, kids that age often feel that way. But it

LA VIDA REAL**105**

didn't take long for me to see that I didn't want to belong to *that*."

To be allowed to leave the gang, Yecenia had to fight her way out, just as she had fought her way in. But this time, the bruises were worth it. It would be the last time Yecenia would fight with her fists and the last time she would flirt with the idea of gang involvement.

When high school began, Yecenia experienced another little bump in the road. When she was given a reading ability test, she was horrified to discover that she was reading at only a fifth-grade level. Although teachers had occasionally commented on her below-average English-speaking skills, they had never mentioned reading or writing problems.

"The schools I was sent to were not very good. I don't think the teachers really cared," Yecenia says honestly. "And I had grown up in a home where my parents only spoke Spanish; they still don't speak very much English at all. As a result, my English was not the best. And on top of that, I obviously couldn't get help from my parents. I ended up taking some ESL classes, and they helped a lot."

And immediately, Yecenia began reading everything she could get her hands on. She was determined to make good grades through high school, but she knew that poor reading ability could hold her back in nearly every subject.

"I read all the time—day and night," Yecenia remembers.

And midway through her freshman English class, Yecenia recalls an unexpected turning point.

"The teacher assigned *Frankenstein* by Mary Shelley. Really, that's not an easy book to read. I had to sit with the book in one hand and a dictionary in the other. When I finished the book, I had to start over and read it all again so that I could really understand it."

But something happened the second time through.

Most people think of *Frankenstein* as being the story of a cruel monster with a stitched-on head who goes around terrorizing people and causing trouble. But that couldn't be further from what the story is truly about. In reality, it is the tale of a lonely and very sad creature. Because of the way he looks, he is unfairly judged by society and hated and feared. He longs for the respect and love that he sees others receiving, but he knows he will never have it.

"I read that book and felt sorry for the monster. I thought of how it was like the Latino community," Yecenia says. "The media really presents us unfairly—whenever you see a Latino person on the news or TV, it's always something negative, something bad. We're often pre-judged. Like when people find out I'm from South Central L.A., they automatically stereotype me, and they know nothing about me."

Sometimes inspiration and fuel for the fire to succeed come from unexpected places. Yecenia credits *Frankenstein* for helping her to see things in a different light. It also helped to give her a love of reading. By the end of her freshman year in high school, she not only had improved her reading by four grade levels; she was setting new and higher goals as well.

"I wanted to make the best grades I could, because I wanted to go to college. More than that, I needed a scholarship since, obviously, our family didn't have the money to pay for college."

Life at Yecenia's high school in South Central was not the easiest. She remembers that drugs were commonplace. Gang tensions and fights were not unusual. Once, a boy who had brought a gun to school fired it accidentally when reaching for a pencil, and he shot a classmate in front of him. And dropping out was more popular than staying in school.

"When I started high school, there were nine hundred students in my freshman class. By the time I graduated, there were fewer than three hundred. The most common reason for dropping out was to get a job to help the family—so many of the students came from backgrounds like mine. So many were poor."

But Yecenia's parents (particularly her father) absolutely refused to let her get a job. The grades were more important. The future—ten, twenty, even thirty years down the line—was even more important. So Yecenia kept her sights on that future and did her best not to let the world around her, the drugs, the violence, the poverty, and the dropouts distract her from her vision. And four years later, she graduated at the top of her class. As her father had demanded, Yecenia had never made a grade lower than an A.

Yecenia was awarded a Gates Millennium Scholarship that covered all four years at the University of California, Los Angeles. Though UCLA is just across town, it was a whole new world for Yecenia.

"Being at UCLA has really made me more aware of diversity," she says. "I was sort of living in my own little world in South Central. You know, for example, I thought all Asian people were the same. I had in my mind how certain groups are. Coming to a big university has made me see the unique differences in people, and it's helped me appreciate those differences."

But college was also hard. It was much harder than high school, and for the first time in her life, Yecenia received a C.

"I was so upset!" she says with a laugh. "It was in physics. I had made an A in physics in high school, so I thought the class would be no problem and that I'd make an A again. Wrong—physics at UCLA was a *lot* harder than it had been at my high school. I realized that I was going to have to work a lot more than I did in high school. I think most students realize that when they get into college. It's a whole different level."

Luckily, Yecenia wasn't majoring in physics. Still, she didn't take an easy path. She chose a double major in history and political science because, as she says, "it's important to know the history of how we got to where we are today. And then it's important to understand what we're doing today. The two majors go hand in hand."

As much work as a double major at UCLA might be, Yecenia still managed to make time to work part time at a law firm *and* volunteer as a director at Project Literacy, a program that helps Latino students between the ages of 6 and 15 with reading and writing skills.

"All of the students have parents who don't speak English. Like it was for me, that is the root of their reading or writing problems." Yecenia thinks about this for a moment and says, "I guess I was destined to become a mentor to these students."

And it is this desire to help others who are in the same position that she was once in that is Yecenia's true passion. Her dream is to open up non-profit programs for literacy, first close to home and then in places as far away as Ethiopia and Central America. But there's a serious plan behind her dream and a determined focus.

"I'll graduate next month, but I'm already applying for law school here at UCLA. It's very difficult to get in, but I'm going to try."

Yecenia's plan involves becoming an entertainment lawyer—a career in which she can make a lot of money, particularly in a place like Los Angeles. Once her career is in place and she's earning a good income—in, say, ten or fifteen years—she plans to start her non-profit literacy programs. In maybe twenty or thirty years, she hopes her efforts will be helping young people around the world. That's a long look into the future for someone who is only 22, but Yecenia thinks that kind of forward thinking is absolutely necessary.

"I always say to the students I mentor, 'Where do you want to be in ten, twenty, thirty years?' Because if they don't think about it or have any kind of plan, they're going to end up just like their parents, working sixty hours a week and earning minimum wage. You *have* to think ahead. You want your own house or a fancy car? You'd better start making a plan."

But then Yecenia backs up for a moment, in the middle of describing future plans, to mention the very first plan she has in place once she has a little money.

"I want to buy my parents a house. We all just moved out of the garage and into a one-bedroom apartment last year since I'm able to help with my part-time job now. But my parents still have to sleep in the living room instead of a bedroom. I want to give them a house before long."

Yecenia is sitting and thinking about all the places she'd like to travel to some day. Sprinkled among the places where she'd like to go to help others are also exciting destinations like France, Spain, and New York City. Yecenia thinks a bit longer and gets a funny grin on her face.

"And the Midwest . . . Kansas," she finally says. Although this seems an odd choice alongside places such as Paris and Buenos Aires, Yecenia has her reasons.

"People always put Kansas down and say, 'Oh, you wouldn't like it. It's too flat,' and so on. But I want to see it and decide for myself. Maybe I'll like it; maybe I won't. But I want to make up my own mind and not judge it before I even see it."

Immediately, Yecenia draws parallels to her own life and the lives of others around her.

"I think that's one of the main reasons a lot of Latinos drop out of school. They get judged by society right from the start. They're kind of told that they'll never amount to anything, so they don't even try. Then they look around, and there aren't very many Latino role models to look up to anyway."

Yecenia thinks about this and frowns. "Younger Latino kids really need someone to look up to."

As Yecenia gathers up her things and heads out the door to squeeze in a few more hours of community service before her next class, she immediately disappears in a crowd of taller students. But it's easy to see that down the road—ten, twenty, and even fifty years from now—Yecenia will be a role model that young people will look up to.

All four feet, eleven inches of her.

Tomas

"A rectangle is drawn on a plane so that its three . . ." Tomas, a strongly built man in his forties, pauses and stumbles over the next word in the book he is reading. "So that its . . . vertices . . . are located at these coordinates. What are the coordinates of the fourth vertex of the angle?"

Tomas looks up from his GED practice book and throws his hands up in the air, laughing and shaking his head.

"See? These questions are impossible! I don't even know what this . . . this . . . *vertices* is. Now, how am I ever going to get a high score on the GED exam?"

But even after saying this, Tomas leans over his worksheet and studies the angles. Scratching away

113

with a stubby pencil and sighing, he fiddles with the numbers and angles for a few minutes. Then, looking up with an expression of sheepish pride, he admits that he thinks he's figured it out.

"To tell you the truth," he says, "some of the math and geometry is not so hard for me. After so many years of bricklaying and construction, some of that stuff is common sense. Figuring out numbers and angles—I think I can do that. But, oh man, the questions about where commas and things go in sentences? There is no way. *No way.*"

At 42, Tomas seems like an unlikely candidate for taking the GED. It makes his goal of doing well on the exam seem even more unusual when you consider that he doesn't really even care about receiving his high-school diploma. Still more curious is the fact that he has no intention of trying to find a better job once he receives his GED.

"I've been working with brick since I was in my twenties, and I am very skilled with it all these years later," Tomas says with a modest smile. "I get paid twenty-five dollars an hour—a lot of money. Some weeks I can get as many hours as I want. So you can see that I have no need for a different job."

After saying this, Tomas gets a kind of guilty look on his face and lowers his voice even though no one else is around.

"My boy, TJ, has quoted me saying that many times. It was his number one excuse for not staying in school, and I can't say that I blame him. You know—if it's good enough for his old man, why isn't it good enough for him? It's a hard thing to explain to a teenage boy because . . ." Tomas thinks for a few seconds, a serious expression on his face.

"Look," he finally says. "There's no shame in hard work, in laying bricks year after year. But there's no glory in it either. That's all right for me, but I want my only son to have more. I want him to have a little glory."

An only child, TJ was raised mostly by his mother, Marie, as his father worked long hours. Both Marie and Tomas had moved to the United States when they were teenagers. They had been boyfriend and girlfriend in their high school in Mexico and left during their senior year to try their luck in the United States. Tomas knew a friend of a friend of a friend who said that *maybe* he could get Tomas on a construction crew. That was good enough for two kids who wanted a change of scenery and some excitement.

Five years later, Tomas and Marie were married with an infant son—Tomas, Jr. ("TJ"). Tomas had worked hard to secure a steady construction job. The only job the original "friend" had found for Tomas was cutting grass for minimum wage. But Tomas never gave up pestering the construction crew bosses for a chance. And finally they gave him one. It was very hot and exhausting working out in the Texas sun all day, but Tomas had his sights set on learning brickwork, and he knew he had to pay his dues doing the "hammer and nail stuff," as he calls it, first. It never crossed his mind to want to return to school. He enjoyed the work he did even if it was tough, and the pay was good.

"I guess sometimes I wondered what I might have been able to do if I'd gotten more learning," Tomas says with a shrug. "You know—maybe I could have been a contractor or owned my own company or something. But I never worried about it. I was happy with what I was doing. I still am."

Even so, like most parents, Tomas wanted something better for his son. And when Marie became sick and then unable to have any more children, Tomas was even more determined that his only child's life would be all that it could be. Tomas dreamed of TJ graduating at the top of his class, getting a scholarship to college, and then going on to be a doctor or a lawyer.

"Yeah, I had a lot of dreams," Tomas says, shaking his head, "but that was about it. Looking back, there were a lot of things I should have been doing to show TJ that I was also interested in education, even though I'd never finished my own. I should have done stuff like read to him when he was younger, or get more involved with his school and teachers and so on. As it is, I just worked long days, came home, and said,

'You better get good grades! You better stay in school!' In the end, it backfired."

Tomas goes on to say that he thinks the root of the problem of kids dropping out of school is their parents.

"People always look at the teenage kids who want to drop out and say, 'We have to do something now to change their minds! We have to fix this right now!' But the problem starts years and years before high school. Parents need to be a lot more involved in their kids' lives and not just say 'do this' and 'do that.' That's the mistake I made."

But this is not to say that TJ had a difficult life. His mother was always at home the entire time he was growing up, and his father earned enough money to give TJ a good home and all the things he needed. That was not true for many of TJ's friends in the mainly Latino part of town where he grew up. Later on, the fact that many of TJ's friends didn't have enough money and wanted to leave school to get jobs would become one of the reasons TJ would lose interest in school himself. But as a young boy, TJ both loved school and was a good student, regardless of his parents' lack of involvement.

"He was extra talented at math and drawing, and he started saying that he wanted to be an architect even back when he was in the 5th grade," Tomas remembers and then adds with a laugh: "He used to point out that he would some day draw the houses that I'd have to build."

As TJ got older, some of his friends began discouraging him from doing his homework and being a good student. They told him that it was a waste of time and that no one needed an education to get a good job. If TJ disagreed, all his friends had to do was point to TJ's own father. Didn't he drop out of high school and still end up with one of the best jobs in the neighborhood? Before long, TJ started cutting classes now and then to go hang out with his friends. And when TJ's best friend dropped out of school completely to get a job to help his family, TJ no longer wanted to stay in school himself.

"It was about this time that TJ started kind of picking at me about how stupid my job was," Tomas says with a sad smile. "I'd fire back and say how great my job was and list all its benefits. If I'd been more in touch with what was going on with my own son at school, I never would have fought back. Obviously, he was just getting reassurance, in a backwards kind of way, that dropping out would be okay."

That was two years ago. TJ quietly began to fade away from school completely, and by the time his parents figured it out (when a report card arrived with mostly F's and "incompletes"), it was too late. TJ had made up his mind to leave school during his senior year and try his luck at a different kind of life.

"Like father, like son, huh?" Tomas says quietly.

Although Tomas begged his son to return to school, TJ refused. He had found a job tinting windows at an auto body shop, and he was already planning how he could work his way up to being a mechanic some day—a job that paid good money. Tomas remained angry and frustrated with his son's behavior until a realization suddenly dawned on him.

"He was copying his old man. At first, I thought he was doing this to be rebellious, but then I realized that he was, in fact, just trying to be like me. He was following my footsteps almost exactly. I'd been a good enough father, I guess. But TJ and I had never been too close—you know, not like friends. This was his way of trying to get closer to me," Tomas says, the emotion showing in his eyes.

So Tomas came up with a plan. He decided to set a "GED Challenge." He would spend a year or so studying and preparing for the GED; then he and TJ would take it on the same day. Whoever got the higher score would win whatever he decided to choose for his prize. TJ decided that he wanted all new rims and tires for his car. But Tomas wanted something quite different.

"I want TJ to go to college," he says with a smile. And then he rolls his eyes. "But I'm already setting aside money to buy his tires. There's no way I'll get a higher score than TJ. He's a really smart kid, and he hasn't been out of high school that long. All this stuff that I'm studying night and day—he already knows it."

But Tomas hopes that the feeling of accomplishment TJ will have when he gets his GED will encourage him to continue his education. He's also betting on the fact that being truly involved in his son's life will turn TJ around. Tomas has begun to bring home materials from the local community college to show TJ the classes in drafting and drawing. It wasn't that long ago that TJ had talked about studying architecture. Tomas knows that interest and talent don't just disappear into thin air. They just need to be re-discovered and encouraged.

Meanwhile, Tomas spends a lot of his spare time bent over the GED practice book, making notes, sighing, and occasionally cursing under his breath. But he works toward his goal, day to day, patiently.

"I look at it like laying bricks," Tomas says with a small laugh. "How else *could* I look at it? But what I mean is this—you see a picture of a finished house, all made of little bricks, and you think, 'Man, that'll take forever. That's impossible.' But then you just start, brick by brick. Then you get closer and closer, until one day, you're done. There's the house."

Tomas thinks about this for a second and smiles.

"But the best part is that, this time, the house I'm building is for my son."